MW00785837

Love and Destiny

Also by Sharon Jeffers

Cards of Destiny: A Birthday Book and Daily Divination Guide

Love and Destiny

Discover the Secret
Language of Relationships

Sharon Jeffers

HAMPTON ROADS
PUBLISHING COMPANY, INC.

Love and Destiny
Discover the Secret Language of Relationships

Sharon Jeffers

Cover design by Steve Amarillo
Cover art and interior card images © MacGregor Historic Games

Hampton Roads Publishing Company, Inc.
1125 Stoney Ridge Road
Charlottesville, VA 22902

434-296-2772
fax: 434-296-5096
e-mail: hrpc@hrpub.com
www.hrpub.com

If you are unable to order this book from your local bookseller,
you may order directly from the publisher.
Call 1-800-766-8009, toll-free.

Library of Congress Cataloging-in-Publication Data

Jeffers, Sharon, 1947-
 Love and destiny : discover the secret language of relationships / Sharon Jeffers.
    p. cm.
 Summary: "A divining method that uses a regular deck of playing cards and a birth date to determine personality types and good/bad relationships"--Provided by publisher.
 ISBN 978-1-57174-590-3 (6.5 x 7.5 hc : alk. paper)
 1. Fortune-telling by cards. 2. Interpersonal relations--Miscellanea. 3. Love--Miscellanea. I. Title.
 BF1878.J45 2008
 133.3'242--dc22
                2008034532

ISBN 978-1-57174-590-3
10 9 8 7 6 5 4 3 2 1
Printed on acid-free paper in China

This book is dedicated to all of humanity.

May we learn to appreciate what
we have been given in one another.

Be fearless in our expression
of love and kindness.

And realize that it's our relationships that bring love, value,
and wisdom into our lives.

And to my beautiful sons,
Spencer and Jonathan, who have taught
me more than they will ever know.

Contents

Acknowledgments

Special thanks to MacGregor Historic Games for the use of its beautiful reproductions of the 16th Century French Playing Cards deck.

Much gratitude to the great team of wonderful people that composes the soulful body of Hampton Roads Publishing Company; thank you for your support, for embracing this project with such enthusiasm, and for creating this beautiful book. Special thanks to Jack Jennings and Greg Brandenburgh, for your interest and insight, and to Jane Hagaman and Tania Seymour, for your warm welcome, artistic sense, great direction, and support.

To Jo Ann Deck, for her kind support and unfaltering guidance in a time when I most needed it, thank you for being there. To Bill Gladstone, for his initial recognition of my work. To Amy Rost, for her insight and skill as an editor, and her willingness to listen for the voice of the oracle. To my dear friends who called and emailed in the final days of this project with encouragement, love, and support. I now believe that it takes a village to write a book, and if I forgot any villagers, please forgive me; I am grateful to all of you.

Tom Johnson, royal salutes to you for your brilliant work with this oracle. I am so grateful for the time we spent together while you were on this planet. You are a true grand master of the Magi. Here's to the relationship book that we almost wrote, my friend. I know you're still here in spirit, and you will be missed. Bless you on your journey.

And, to my beloved son Spencer, who through his journey here and in spirit has brought me to be where I am in my life. You carried me to my destiny. I love you and I miss you beyond what words can say. To my one and only Jon, you are a magnificent son and I am so blessed to have you in my life. Thank you for your love, support, and unending wisdom. Please keep me laughing until I die.

To the Order of the Magi—you certainly make your agendas clear, one way or another. I am eternally grateful for the opportunity. Thank you.

Introduction

*It's so easy to feel alone sometimes, we try to fit in each other's
dreams, but somehow I know there's a real connection, soaring so
deep, inside you and me.*

—From the song "It's a Real Love"
by Fuzzbee Morris and Kim O'Leary

What is it that drives us to be in relationship? Is it the need to be loved? Is it a need to love another? Is it both? Is it because we feel empty when we're alone? Or is it simply that we are meant to share our lives intimately with others so that we have someone to bear witness to that fact that we actually exist?

Within each one of us there is a tendency to think of ourselves as being alone and separate from the rest of the world. The great philosophers, spiritual teachers, and quantum physicists tell us differently. The collective agreement of the higher minds of humanity suggests that we all are one and that, indeed, we all are connected. If this is so, is it then our limited perceptions and unconscious beliefs that keep us from embracing our oneness with humanity and life itself? Is it our lack of this awareness that causes our loneliness and feelings of separation? And is it loneliness that motivates us to make uninformed, unconscious decisions regarding our relationship choices? Perhaps the answer to all of these questions is *yes*.

In presenting the material in this book, I do not profess to be a relationship expert. I'm not a therapist, nor do I have a degree in relationship counseling. I am, however, someone who has been blessed and gifted with profound knowledge from an ancient source of wisdom that reveals the most significant insights that we can have regarding our connections with one another—why they exist, what they bring to us, and what can be found within them.

I have worked with thousands of people, facilitating their personal transformation, for more than twenty-five years. In my studies I have learned and applied some of the profound methodologies, such as applied kinesiology, light therapy, behavior and educational kinesiology, numerology, and astrology. I've worked with young children and parents, kids at risk and prison inmates, police academy instructors, teachers, corporations, health institutions, and celebrities. In all my years of training, teaching, and facilitating, and with all that I have done, all of which has been very valuable, the information that I share in this book is, to me, the most important thing for me to share at this time in my life. I value this ancient system because it reveals precisely who we are as individuals and as a whole as humanity, what our destiny is in life, and who we are when we're in relationship with one another.

The information in these pages is a small fraction of a mystical science gifted to humanity by the Ancient Order of the Magi. This ancient system has changed my life and the lives of others. Knowing and understanding, first, who we are and the energetic composition that we embody as individuals and, second, how that energy transforms to express itself when we are with another can give us amazing insights into our relationships. As you read on, may you be delighted as you discover the secret language that has been whispering in our ears for a very long time. And may you be empowered to see yourself and others with greater wisdom, understanding, and compassion.

Endless gratitude to the Ancient Order of the Magi.

Many blessings to all of us.

Sharon Jeffers

The Hidden Conversations in Our Relationships

Man is a knot into which relationships are tied.

—Antoine de Saint-Exupéry, *Flight to Arras*
(translated from French by Lewis Galantière)

We've all experienced feeling a certain way with one person and completely different with another. With one person we may show one side of our personality, and with another we experience just the opposite. With one individual we are inspired, and with another left feeling stifled. We are excited and attracted to one person, and then have the exact opposite reaction to somebody else. What changes? Do we change with each person we're with? Or is it the dynamics created with another person that change with each individual we encounter? What motivates our behaviors and the ways we choose to communicate with each individual we connect with?

And how closely do we pay attention to the subtleties of our interactions with one another? We may witness these dynamics in varying degrees, but how often do we stop and think about what's actually taking place or, more importantly, why these variations in our behaviors, interactions, and feelings are happening at all?

The Chemistry of Love

The meeting of two personalities is like the contact of two chemical substances if there is any reaction, both are transformed.

—Carl Jung

When we come together with another person, a third entity is formed, and we call this entity "a relationship." What most of us may not be aware of is that relationships are living, breathing personifications of energy. Each relationship has its own distinct personality. It embodies its own brand of challenges and opportunities, and it has a life path and a destiny. A relationship has a temperament and preferences, and it is filled with specific intentions for its self-expression. When we enter into a relationship, we step into an invisible cosmic bubble that's filled with the substance of its own intelligence and its own agendas. The influences that exist within the domain of the relationship immediately began to interact with each of us as individuals, and those influences have undeniable and profound effects on our personal awareness and our interactions with one another. When attraction and magnetism show up between us and another person, and we step into an intimate relationship, many unseen dynamics are stirred into the recipe that we have named love. These dynamics can be intense at times and mysterious at others.

The Reflections of Our Soul

Love is, above all else, the gift of oneself.

—Jean Anouilh

Mirror, mirror on the wall, am I seeing me at all?
Relationships are our mirrors, and we must remain open and pay

attention to what we see in them. Those we love, those we encounter, and those we desire are reflections that enable us to see with greater clarity not only who we are, but also the dynamics that are occurring within our own heads and hearts. Just as the eyes are the windows of the soul, our relationships are the windows to our inner world and the most important and most primary relationship of all: the one we have with our self. When we see something in a partner, friend, or loved one that causes us to react, we are being given the opportunity to turn inward and look at the scenario that's playing out within our subconscious.

For most of us, relationships are a major part of our lives. They add depth and meaning to our experiences, they stir the pot of our emotions, and they take us to places within our self where we might not otherwise go on our own. They challenge us, and they nurture us; they make demands of us, and they bless us. Relationships are the most powerful initiators of change that exist for us as human beings. We are attracted to and draw others to us for a reason, always. Each person we come into contact with has a gift to give us, a gift to receive from us, or both. Each person brings us lessons to be learned and opportunities for our personal growth. The people we bring into our lives are our teachers and mirrors, and when we see them in this way and are curious and grateful, we can see the magic of life playing with us through our connections with others.

The secret to relationship success lies in understanding ourselves first, then the person we are in relationship with, and finally the dynamics that are created when we come together with that person in a relationship.

What if we could understand the invisible dynamics that govern each one of our relationships? What if we could see exactly what the relationships mean, what our learning is, what the gifts and strengths are, what the challenges are, and perhaps why we have chosen them? What if we had a way to see exactly what's going on in a relationship with someone and why we feel one way with one person and another with someone else? It would be exceedingly helpful, insightful, and empowering.

There are many tools, bodies of knowledge, and techniques that focus on relationship compatibility. Some examples would be the various schools of astrology and numerology that observe the dynamics between two people with great accuracy. In the realms of traditional therapy, the focus is on the psychological dynamics between people and the individuals' personal issues that show up in their relationships. All of these bodies of wisdom are important for the development of self-understanding and the cultivation of a partnership; however, there's something being overlooked if we stop there. There's another school of wisdom that reveals something more—something very significant that, when understood, can enlighten us and liberate us to greater self-awareness and understanding, and empower us to have happier, more successful relationships in our lives.

There is a hidden language in relationships, and this secret language is defined and revealed in an ancient little book of wisdom. This little book was originally used as a map of humankind's journey through time, of our destinies as they unfold, and to the meaning of our personal relationships with one another. This little book, given to humanity by an ancient order of magi, is designed to guide us through time, show us who we really are, describe what life has to offer each of us as individuals, and direct us on our paths of self-mastery. In the realm of relationships, I have seen nothing else that so specifically reveals the hidden influences that are at work in our relationships with other human beings.

This sacred language comes from an ancient science, and the little book of wisdom that I speak of is actually the deck of playing cards.

The Secrets of the Ancients

Destiny grants us our wishes, but in its own way, in order to give us something beyond our wishes.

—Johann Wolfgang von Goethe

If you are new to this mystic science of the cards, welcome to an amazing oracle that reveals the structure of time and where we are in our journey as we move through time. This ancient body of wisdom also gives us greater insight to who we are, what we innately bring into this experience we call life, and the dynamics that exist within our relationships.

I first came upon this system in 1990 while perusing a metaphysical bookstore in the San Fernando Valley of southern California. I knew there was something in that store for me, and when I found it, I felt like I had been reunited with a very dear old friend. It was this oracle. The book I joined with on that day was *The Sacred Symbols of the Ancients,* published in 1947. As I wandered through its pages, I knew I was being reminded of something that I, for sure, had known a long time ago.

It was some time before I began writing about the oracle in my own words, and as I embarked upon that journey, I was amazed at how the cards continuously revealed their wisdom to me. The accuracy that I found hidden within the sacred symbols of the card deck was nothing short of impressive. I soon discovered that, in addition to keeping time and making predictions with amazing accuracy, this system, when applied to relationships, was unsurpassed in its delineations of the character and nature of our connections with one another. Some of those connections are dreamy and juicy, some are difficult and filled with challenges, and some are powerful in their ability to further define our character and our creative expression. The learning potential within the connections we have with others is vast and varied, and using this oracle to observe the invisible influences at work in a relationship is a powerful way to gain insight and understanding of our relationships and ourselves.

Unveiling the Intention of Time

In ancient times, in many civilizations, it was recognized that time has intention. Each day carried a name, and that name was filled with meaning—a destiny, if you will. In some cultures, a child was given the name of the day he or she was born on, and everyone understood that the child embodied the energy of that day for his or her entire lifetime. Our civilization has lost touch with many things, including any acknowledgment of the meaning of time that we might have had. We have entered a collective unconscious agreement of what time is and how time is structured. We don't question that it's Tuesday, or August, or 2008.

The ancient system of the cards shows the intention of each day of the year. Interestingly, the deck of cards corresponds with our current Gregorian calendar in several key ways. There are:

52 cards and 52 weeks in the year

12 court cards (jacks, queens, kings) in a deck and 12 months in a year

4 suits (hearts, clubs, diamonds, spades) in a deck and 4 seasons in a year

13 cards in each suit (ace through king), 13 weeks in each season, and 13 lunar cycles in the year

7 cycles of 52 days in a year and 7 days in the week

When you add all the cards together by the number of pips on the card (1+2+3, etc., through the entire deck) the sum total is 364. Add the Joker, and the final sum is 365, the number of days in the calendar year.

Furthermore, this ancient system defines the intention that time has for each of us personally, day by day and year by year, from our birth onward. Imagine, all the while we've been playing with the deck of cards, we've been holding in our hands the secret of how our lives inherently unfold through time. We've also been holding onto the keys that unlock the secret language that is hidden within our relationships.

This system is a most excellent tool for determining relationship compatibility. When I speak of compatibility, I am not referring to whether or not we are compatible; I am referring to the discovery of how it is that we are compatible with one another.

As each day of the calendar year is governed by a specific card (see the chart titled "What's Your Card?"), the day we were born on determines our birth card. Following the birth card, there are twelve additional cards that form a thirteen-card personal life path for each one of us. Every one of those thirteen cards represents a significant influence and/or specific cycle of time throughout our life. Our personal life path defines who we are and where we are in time, including the many cycles that we have throughout our lives. The details revealed by this mystic science are uncanny in their precision.

Our Connections Are Sacred

When you step into relating with me, fresh dynamics come into play within each of us and between the two of us. These dynamics are filled with intention. These intentions emerge from the combination of the sacred symbols and numeric energies that compose each of the cards. Every one of the cards embodies special traits, wisdom, challenges, and gifts. Each connection is sacred in that it embodies its own special gift of wisdom, which is there for us to discover as individuals in relationship together. The compatibility reports for each of the composite cards define, one by one, the energetic compositions of our relationships.

The focus of this book is on the cards that govern the relationship itself, the energies each card will evoke, and the potential of the relationship in general. In addition to finding the composite cards of a relationship, as described in "The Relationship Reading" section, there is another way to gain insight through these relationship composites. If your birth card is a Jack of Diamonds, you can read the Jack of Diamonds compatibility report to more deeply understand how the Jack of Diamonds behaves when in a relationship. Apply the wisdom of the cards that you find in this book, and your awareness of yourself, your partner, and your relationship will be enhanced. If you are looking for a relationship, or if you're dating, you can use this information to know in advance what a relationship is going to be like and whether or not it's the best choice for you.

Some composite cards indicate an extremely challenging relationship. I do tell you to think twice about these connections. I think that it's important to be realistic in regard to our relationships with one another. Fantasy rules strongly over the heart and mind when romance steps onto the dance floor. Fantasy is wonderful and deliciously delightful to indulge in. However, it's not the best foundation for making important decisions regarding life or relationships. Understanding the dynamics of these composite cards can bring tremendous insight and guidance, which will lead to stronger bonds of love, deeper and more meaningful experiences in communication, greater self-learning, and enhanced self-awareness.

The Relationship Reading

When this system is applied to relationship compatibility, it yields multiple layers of information. One of the many amazing aspects of this ancient system is how accurately it defines relationship dynamics. Not only does it define them, but it also enlightens us to what those dynamics are in a more conscious way. It gives us the wisdom to determine how to interface with the influences that govern our connections with one another, so that we can choose how to interact from a more informed state of mind. The more we learn about ourselves and how these dynamics work, the more success we will have in our relationships and in our lives in general. It's quite amazing to experience how clearly and accurately the cards define our relationships. It really is quite profound.

The Four Personal Significators

Four primary cards, referred to as personal significators, are taken from the thirteen cards that compose each individual person's life path. These four personal significators are the birth card, the spirit card, the planetary ruling card, and the soul card.

Your Birth Card

Determined by the month and day you were born, the birth card represents your soul's expression in this life. The influences of this card manifest as your distinguishing signature to be expressed to the world. It's like the costume you are wearing to the ball. You personify the essence of this card as an expression of self, and you identify with it deeply on the subconscious level. Your lessons are embodied in the life path of your birth card.

Your Spirit Card

This card represents the inner environment of your psyche and what you deal with inside your own mind. This is an aspect of yourself that wants to experience the fulfillment of self-expression. This card carries your challenges and your opportunities relative to self-expression; when you embrace and resolve the challenges specific to this card's true desires, the challenges transform and become your rewards. We are happiest when we are expressing the full potential of our spirit card.

Your Planetary Ruling Card

This is the card in your life path that corresponds with the ruling planet of your astrological sign. You identify with this card's influence on the mental level and act out its characteristics. This card is like an overlay of traits and characteristics in your personality; we often think that this is who we are. In your life path, this card has to do with your karmic journey and represents how others perceive you. The characteristics of this card show up clearly in how we move through the world.

Your Soul Card

This card embodies the gifts that the wisdom of your soul has brought into this life with you, and it guides you as to how to use those gifts to manifest the essence of who you really are. The soul card reveals where you have come from as an individual, and it is the representative of your soul's true essence and nature. This card is a guiding force that reveals your preferred path for expressing your essential wisdom, be it through the work that you do or how you give back to life.

In the back of the book, you will find reference charts that will enable you to determine your personal spirit, soul, and planetary ruling cards. You can learn more about the essence of your birth card and your other personal significators in my book *Cards of Destiny,* which delineates all fifty-three cards and the characteristics they bring forth in each of us as individuals.

Relationship Composite Cards

As mentioned earlier, a relationship consists of three components: you, the other person, and the relationship itself. Each one of those three components has a life path in the cards. As individuals, we embody the characteristics of the cards that create our personal life path. The result of combining our cards with another's is a unique expression that can only come from that particular combination of cards. When our personal cards are combined with the cards of another person, the cards they create are referred to as **composite cards.** The composite cards then become the governing influences of the relationship and determine its life path.

For a relationship reading, I recommend finding composites for all four personal significators (birth, spirit, soul, and planetary ruling cards). That way you are gaining insight into the relationship from four unique and very important perspectives. Each combination will determine the specific characteristics and the life path of your relationship. I suggest combining birth card and birth card, spirit card and spirit card, soul card and soul card, and planetary ruling card and planetary ruling card to explore the influences of all four of those important significators and the specific ways in which they govern the relationship.

When the two birth cards are combined, the **birth composite card** that comes forth determines the life path of the relationship and embodies the soul's expression of the relationship. The birth composite card of the relationship also determines the life cycles of the relationship relative to time, the lessons that are present to be learned, and the expressions the relationship will bring forth in each person. This composite card represents the dominating influence of the relationship. It is the one that defines the life path of your connection and time together.

The **spirit composite card** shapes the inner life of the relationship. It determines the challenges and opportunities that exist. When the challenges are embraced, the opportunities emerge as blessings. As time goes on and you become more aware of how these challenges show up in the relationship, you will learn to embrace them as opportunities, turning the challenges into freedom of personal expression, which will take the relationship to a new level of greatness and, by giving you greater awareness, attune each of you to your passion.

The **planetary ruling composite card** will reveal how others perceive your relationship and how the two of you move through the world as a couple. This card also determines the mental environment of your connection and how each of you perceives the relationship. This card presents a map of the relationship's karmic journey and can present insightful glimpses into your personalities.

The **soul composite card** will reveal the gifts that the relationship has for you. It will give you guidance about the most auspicious path your relationship can be on and will support each of you in expressing your gifts to the world. The soul composite card is your spiritual guide.

How to Find Your Relationship Composite Cards

Each of the fifty-two cards in the deck has what is known as a solar value, which is a numeric value that is assigned to the card. For example, the Ace of Hearts has a solar value of 1, and the King of Spades has a solar value of 52. The solar values of the deck follow a specific order in number and suit from the first card, which is the Ace of Hearts, through the heart suit, club suit, diamond suit, and spade suit to the final card, the King of Spades. The numeric values of the cards can be found in the solar values chart in the back of the book.

A composite (relationship) card is determined by adding the solar values of two or more cards together. I say "two or more" because sometimes there are more than two people relating together. An example of this threefold relationship would be a couple that have a child. Before the child arrives, the composite cards of the couple are determined by adding together the solar values of each individual's significator cards. The resulting composite cards define the life path of the couple's relationship. When a child comes into the picture, we then add the solar value of the child's card to that of the parents' cards, yielding a new composite card that reflects the changes in the dynamics of the family relationship. Relationship dynamics change every time a new element (person) is added. This principle applies to every type of relationship, with varying numbers of people; whether it is in family dynamics, work dynamics, classroom dynamics—it doesn't matter. When doing composites for the dynamics of the entire family, you would add the solar values of all the family members' cards together. It's very revealing.

Here's an example: Jane's birth card is the Four of Clubs (4♣). The solar value (SV) of the Four of Clubs is 17. Her husband Frank's birth card is a Nine of Hearts (9♥). The SV of the Nine of Hearts is 9. To find the composite of these two cards, which is the card that governs their relationship, we add 9 and 17 for a total of 26. Then we look at the solar values chart to see which card has 26 as its SV, and that would be the King of Clubs. So the card that governs Jane and Frank's relationship is the King of Clubs.

4♣ = 17

9♥ = 9

17 + 9 = 26

SV 26 = K♣ = composite card for the relationship.

Note: If, when you add the solar values of two cards together, the total is more than 52, you then subtract 52 from your total until your sum total is 52 or less. There are only 52 solar values. For example, the Jack of Diamonds (J♦) has a SV of 37. The Four of Spades (4♠) has a SV of 43. Adding these solar values together gives us a total of 80. There is no card with a solar value of 80, so we subtract 52 from 80, leaving a total of 28. The card with the SV of 28, and the composite card for this relationship, is the Two of Diamonds (2♦).

J♦ = 37

4♠ = 43

37 + 43 = 80

80 − 52 = 28

SV 28 = 2♦

In their relationship together, Frank and Jane are strongly influenced by the energy of the King of Clubs, which is the birth composite card of their relationship. Now comes the baby, and he's a Six of Clubs (6♣). How does the dynamic of the family change? We add the SV of the King of Clubs (26), which is the governing card of Jane and Frank's connection, with that of the baby's, which is the Six of Clubs (19) and get a new SV of 45, which is the Six of Spades (6♠). The family dynamic has now gone from a King of Clubs to a Six of Spades, which is quite a shift, actually. When Jane and Frank are alone together, they are still under their powerful, individualistic King of Clubs umbrella; when baby joins in, the dynamic changes to the dreamier Six of Spades.

K♣ = 26 = pre-baby relationship composite card

6♣ = 19 = baby's birth card

26 + 19 = 45

SV 45 = 6♠

When using the Joker birthday (December 31) in your calculations, the solar value will be 53. If 53 is the sum total of a composite calculation, you can look at both the Joker and the Ace of Hearts as governing influences for the connection.

In addition to composite cards, there are planetary influences and aspects within our individual life paths that explain how we relate to one another. These dynamics are a bit different in how they show up in a relationship, and they are found through reading the life paths of the two individuals. The composite cards, however, which are what the compatibility reports in this book are based on, are the specific cards that govern the relationship itself.

The Sacred Symbols

This oracle empowers us to be in command of our personal kingdom and teaches us how to do so. The symbols of the deck reveal our path to self-mastery, our truest expressions of passion, the secrets to using our personal power to manifest in our lives, and the knowledge of our innate wisdom, whether we are conscious of it or not. They reveal the true secret, which is that we actually are the secret—each and every one of us—and that we already embody the power and wherewithal to create our realities, as we've been doing since the beginning of time. Life is expressed through co-creation. We refer to this expression as manifestation. The art of manifestation is not a singular experience. It's the result of a joint articulation, which comes from our intentional relationship and communication with the intelligence of life. This oracle is a road map of who and where we are, and of the influences that govern us in the fourth dimension of time as we move through it from birth to death.

I want to begin by sharing the right order of the suits, which is hearts ♥, clubs ♣, diamonds ♦, and spades ♠, and their relationship to time relative to the evolution of humanity.

♥ Hearts represent conception, birth, childhood, youth, family, and the beginning of life.

♣ Clubs represent our time of education, the gathering of information, and learning of the world.

♦ Diamonds represent our values and our personal expressions and our time of manifesting.

♠ Spades represent the later years in our life, our spirituality, wisdom, and determination.

Each suit is more thoroughly defined in the following pages. I highly recommend that as you read their definitions, you think about people you know and the suits of their birth cards, so you can begin observing how they express being a heart, a club, a diamond, or a spade. I promise you that it will be both fascinating and highly informative. Also start thinking of yourself as a heart, a club, a diamond, or a spade. The cards are not two-dimensional; they are dynamic, living expressions of the secrets that are hidden behind the veil of life.

♥ The Heart Suit: Springtime and the First Season of Life

The heart suit symbolizes the springtime of life and the element of fire. It represents the source of beginning, childhood, and family. Hearts relate to art and beauty, feelings and emotions, youth and children, people and relationships, as well as love, marriage, and home. This suit characterizes the passion of fire tamed through compassion. Hearts symbolize all things that touch our emotions and cause us to feel, such things as devotion and passion. The awakened heart embodies love, compassion, understanding, and kindness, and he or she is giving and kind. The unawakened heart can become lost in drama, challenged by lust, addiction, anger, promiscuity, and self-absorption. This suit represents the time of life when we learn through our emotional environment, by way of our feelings and our close relationships. We learn to how to be in relationship with ourselves, and the world around us, through the experiences we have with our families, our friends, and our earliest encounters with people. It is during this time in life that our inner emotional environments are established. The symbol of the heart represents two who have become one in their embrace.

Those who are born in the heart suit process their experiences of life through their emotions, their feelings, and their interactions with others. When they communicate, the information shared goes through their "feeling" filter first and then to wherever else it may apply to them mentally. In the calendar, the heart birthdays begin to show their lovely faces on June 30 and continue through to December 30.

♥ The Heart-Governed Relationship

Heart-governed relationships teach us the true laws of love, as the highest law of the heart is compassion. If love goes sour, it turns to lust, jealousy, self-pity, self-indulgence, and even meanness. Selfless giving is the true way and highest expression of the heart. It is through giving that we receive our rewards and the gifts that life chooses to give to us. In a heart-governed relationship, the danger lies in becoming self-absorbed or codependent, and in having expectations regarding what we think we should have or deserve, or what we think someone else should be giving to us, rather then focusing on what we can give. When we choose this path, we create sour love. It's like putting lemon into milk. The milk curdles, and so do we. Heart-ruled relationships, at their finest, are yummy, juicy, and filled with joy, sensuality, and greatness. The lessons brought forth in these relationships center around the wisdom that occurs from giving rather than getting. Heart-governed relationships can be some of the most wonderful connections in the deck, since the cards in this suit are the rulers of love.

♣ The Club Suit: Summertime and the Second Season of Life

Clubs rule the mental realm and all things having to do with the mind and its expressions. Education, communication, writing, self-expression, research, teaching, lecturing, psychology, publishing— all exist within the realm of the club's domain. This suit is related to summer and the element of air, and, in our journey through life, the time when we become educated and grow—the time when we gather information and learn from the world around us through communication and our perception. Clubs represent the union of Heaven and Earth, or the mind of God and the mind of humankind, through the integration of the higher mind with the mundane. The symbol of the club suit, the shamrock, represents the expression of the knowledge of science, art, and spirituality—all being initiated through the intelligence of life and planted in the mind of humanity through its stem as it founds itself in the earthly plane.

For those born with club birthdays, thoughts are real and tangible—like objects. Their greatest quest is for universal knowledge, and they are unrelenting in their gathering of information. Thoughts are the building blocks of understanding and design the construction of conceptual frameworks. These people are the guardians of intelligence. The danger for the club person lies in becoming trapped in his or her own mental structures to the point of being stuck or myopic in attitude or point of view. When unaware, the club person can be extremely aggressive, unreliable, and dishonest—behaviors that are based in fear. The brilliant side of the club suit, and those who have these birthdays, is the manifestation and expression of pure creative mental energy, natural intelligence, and intuition. Those born with these birthdays are highly creative, magnetic, and dynamic in their self-expression.

♣ The Club-Governed Relationship

Relationships that are governed by the club suit rely on clear and thorough communication for mental and emotional stability. Communication is the key to security, stability, and success. Self-expression is extremely important for each person in the relationship, as is harmony in the environment. Any and all of the elements that foster a peaceful environment for the mind will be important in a club relationship. Fear and uncertainty will be the culprits that test the certainty of each individual's mind in a club relationship, which is why it's absolutely necessary for both parties in the relationship to be expressive and communicative, especially of feelings. Whether you're a heart, diamond, or spade by birth, being in a club relationship will bring out the mental qualities of the connection with your partner, for better or worse. So the more you understand these influences and dynamics, the better informed you will be and able to make the appropriate choices in your communication. The danger that lies in a club relationship will always be found in the choice to argue, or be "right," rather than going beyond personal fears to initiate communication from the feelings, which the club nature can tend to avoid.

◆ The Diamond Suit: Autumn and the Third Season of Life

Diamonds stand for values, worth, and money. They are associated with autumn and the harvest of life and with the element of water. In our journey through time, diamonds represent the manifestation of our passion and what we have learned, and, as such, they are action oriented. This is the time in our journey when we give back to life and receive the treasures that life has to give us. This is the time when we sow and reap. Diamonds represent both spiritual and material substance. Light actually passes through the precious stones we call diamonds. The light that passes through the physical diamond is a metaphor for the responsibility to higher spiritual and material values that is asked of the diamond person or people in a diamond-ruled relationship. When we don't assume the higher reasonability of this suit, we become consumed with deceit, greed, and selfishness. Where the heart person chooses to feel and the club person chooses to think, the diamond person takes action. The most auspicious action comes from sound values, which are the foundation, good or bad, of how we choose to live our lives each moment. Creating abundance for others is the highest order of this suit. The symbol of the diamond represents the merging of the highest values from above to secure them in the Earth plane below. The diamond symbolizes the infusion of light into the mundane mind of humanity.

For those with diamond birthdays, money, value, and worth are issues that are at the forefront of every endeavor, whether it is personal or professional. Choices are made according to the value something—or someone—will bring. Action is the key word for diamond people. The diamond naturally understands the value of action and what is possible when you move your thoughts forward in practical ways to bring them into form. The danger for the diamond person lies in not taking the time to think things through thoroughly. On the high side, diamonds are generous and can wield tremendous power for the abundance and goodness of others and themselves. The unenlightened diamond can be obsessed with material gain to the point of greed and gain nothing of value in return. The diamond suit governs manifestation in the earthly plane.

◆ The Diamond-Governed Relationship

These relationships are, of course, based on value and worth. These attributes are understandably important for all relationships, but they are imperative in a diamond relationship. Being in a diamond relationship will bring up an individual's issues regarding self-worth and value. When a diamond connection is shared, partners must have like values. Values are a major focus for these relationships, and this principle will apply whether those in the relationship are aware of it or not, so intentions and integrity will be in the spotlight. Working together can be lucrative, especially if you are creative in your endeavors. Because diamonds are action oriented, moving forward on projects together, being strong in your individuality, and being generous with your giving are the keys to having a successful relationship. There can be a bit of an edge in these connections, so it's important to value your partner first and foremost, as the diamond ruling cards will bring forth the need for acknowledgment and appreciation. These relationships can also be in the limelight or in public as they seem destined to attract attention, for better or worse.

♠ The Spade Suit: Wintertime and the Fourth Season of Life

Spades are associated with the wintertime and the element of earth. This is the suit of the initiate and our time to turn to our inner source of wisdom. This suit represents spirituality, health, work, labor, determination, and discipline. In the greater cycle of time, spades represent our later years, when we walk hand in hand with life as our teacher and we look beyond our own ideas to gain greater insight. This is the time when we integrate our emotional experiences with the knowledge we have gained, and we apply our values and our discovery of what is worthy of our time to become wise. Spades are the fourth and final suit in the deck; following the passion of nature to create (hearts), the creative intelligence of life (clubs), and the blessings of life's riches through experience (diamonds) comes the final command to find excellence through wisdom and to bring forth the re-creation and rebirth of life to begin again.

Those with spade birthdays tend to be more serious about things than the rest of us. They innately understand the cycles of birth, death, and rebirth, as this innate wisdom resides deep within the fabric of their being. They're not afraid of hard work or of commitment to things that take time. Putting the shoulder to the grindstone comes all too easily to the spade person. Spirituality and wisdom are their driving forces. Intelligence is greatly appreciated. As Edith Randall said, "They are the diggers of truth." And they are. They seek to find the wisdom that is hidden in life, and they tire not in the process. The Ace of Spades—the keeper of secrets and mysteries—represents this oracle. The King of Spades, who is the final card and king of kings in the deck, represents material and spiritual self-mastery. The symbol of the spade suit unites the sword and the acorn, representing the unending cycles of death and rebirth.

♠ The Spade-Governed Relationship

Personally, I think it's important to have a spiritual connection at the foundation of a spade relationship. It's vital for these relationships to include shared values; religious beliefs; spiritual practices; work in the healing arts, medicine, or law; or at least an understanding of one or more of these things. These relationships bring us into a more grounded state of being as individuals; they encourage practical thinking. There can sometimes be challenges or times when things seem to take more effort than they otherwise would. Often these are times for greater self-discipline and determination. Spades are the teachers of self-discipline and the importance of determination. Spade relationships can be very solid, are often oriented toward work or spirituality, and can bring out the best in us when we apply our efforts toward personal self-mastery. The danger for the spade relationship lies in becoming stuck in fixed attitudes or behaviors, which can lead to stagnation and boredom.

Each of the suits represents a time in the life of humanity and a cycle of development in our own personal evolution as individuals. The four suits are the keepers of wisdom and teachers of knowledge, whether that knowledge be of the heart, the mind, the body, or the spirit; the four cycles of life can come about multiple times in a single day, and when we are willing to be present and aware to observe them, we can learn what it is they have to teach. A suit and specific cards govern each day of the year. These influences exist to ignite our desire to become more consciously aware and present in our lives. Paying attention to their teachings can quicken our journey in self-awareness.

The Power of Numbers

In addition to being governed by one of the four suits, each relationship is governed by a numeric influence. The numbers can be seen as living entities, and the greater your understanding of their "personalities," the more empowered you will be in your understanding of your connections with others. A scholar of math will tell you that the universe can be completely defined through mathematics, so here we will apply that science to the art of relating, from ace (1) to king (13).

Aces are self-motivated and self-focused. The energy of the ace is aggressive, forward moving, driven by desire, and often selfish. The ace embodies strong characteristics of leadership, and those with ace birth cards are great initiators. Aces are naturally driven by desire, and when this fast-moving energy is the governing influence in a relationship, it will be important to gain clarity when making decisions and be sure you are realistic about what is motivating you to make those choices. At times, desire can be so strong with this energy that it moves us before we actually know why we are being moved or why we are going in the directions we have taken, which can lead to poor choices and reckless behaviors. For these reasons, it's extremely important to be aware of and attentive to details when making important decisions.

In ace-governed relationships, our individuality and our independence are drawn forth to fuller expression, and enhancing those aspects of our personalities becomes a theme for greater self-awareness. Each person's individual expression and desire for independence become more pronounced in these relationships. People born on ace birthdays are often visionaries. When one of the four aces is the composite card of a relationship, the dreamer or the visionary will be awakened in each person. When we're under this influence, we almost always need to make greater efforts regarding the needs of the other person; we also need to make a conscious effort toward greater awareness and efforts to listen and be open and receptive. The learning in an ace relationship is all about self-awareness and knowing the difference between honoring your individuality and being selfish and thought-less.

Two represents communication, cooperation, and communion. The danger for individuals whose birth card is a two is in becoming codependent or passive. In a two relationship, communication is not only favored, but it's also exalted. So talking and sharing become a foundation of strength and are often the most shared experiences for this connection. The number two represents relationship, and two-governed relationships are often long lasting and have constant growth and learning opportunities in the area of communication and sharing. There can be wonderful connectedness, harmony, and love in these connections. The area of challenge in a two relationship is fear, which switches on the survival reflexes and leads to arguments and confrontations. The secret to unlocking and eliminating fear is through deepening your connection with one another. Communication from the heart, with clarity and intention and for the purpose of seeking wisdom and harmony, will always be the magic doorway of these relationships.

Three is the number of creativity and expression. The stable expression of the three is present when we are channeling our creative intelligence in some way, whether it is through the arts, business, a hobby, or community service. It doesn't matter how we channel it; it just matters that we do, because when we are not channeling this energy in some way, be it mental or physical, it can turn into indecision, confusion, or insecurity that leads the mind into utter chaos.

Relationships governed by the number three can feel unstable and create questions and underlying feelings of uncertainty. It's important to recognize and honor the heightened sensitivity that can occur in people who are engaged in relationships governed by the number three. These relationships need to be kept light, loving, and liberating for both parties. When emotions feel uncertain, an opportunity is presenting itself. That opportunity is to lighten up, move the body, and engage in physical activities alone and together. This is wonderful, playful energy that can encourage innocence and new explorations of self-expression.

Four is the number of form and stability. Four brings love, ideas, values, and the unknown into form. Four builds stability and creates containment. The challenge for four lies in becoming stuck in ideas or routines in ways that cause stagnation or in choosing stubborn behaviors or rigid attitudes.

In a relationship, the four's energy establishes strong foundations for love to grow on and creates solid structures of stability and longevity. The danger occurs when one becomes too fixed in attitudes or stuck in routines, and measures should be taken to keep these things from happening. On the cheerful side of things, four-based relationships are some of the most stable in the deck, and much goodness and good fortune can be built and enjoyed with these connections.

Five represents change and adaptation. Whatever can change is bound to with this connection. Whatever can move absolutely will. Adventure and variety have to be high on the priority list. New things will be sought, resulting in changes in thought, values, and self-expression. Restlessness will be present when movement and exploration are not given priority. Embedded in the energy of the five is the duty to shake things up a bit with the intention of bringing new perspectives and experiences to the individual and to humankind in general. In a partnership, it will bring about change time and time again.

In a relationship, this energy can be a wild ride for sure, and the relationship will be one that is full of life, variety, fun, and adventure.

Here, the danger lies in not fulfilling this energy's desire to explore and discover, which will result in restlessness and boredom, and eventually will begin deteriorating the fabric of the connection. Adventures, activities, and variety are absolutely necessary for a five relationship to be a happy one. Much can be explored and discovered in these relationships.

Six represents balance and harmony, and it is a very nice number for a relationship, as long as we avoid getting into argumentative ego battles with one another. When these battles occur, we need to recognize them and make a choice to behave differently. Sixes can be very stubborn. Changes in behavior will result when attitudes are shifted from stubborn to flexible. The six-based connections teach us a great deal about the importance of emotional balance and harmony, and bring us opportunities to learn these lessons through the surrender of our egos.

Life can be dreamy within a six connection, so it's important that we maintain a realistic point of view. Most often the world is viewed through rose-colored glasses. The problem arises when the glasses fall off and reality shows up in ways that we were oblivious to. This is when the ego battles begin. Another common dynamic is that of lethargy, or being more lax than what is appropriate to cause things to happen in our lives. In a six relationship, we must dream together and engage our imaginations, and then take action with our visions to ensure that the life of the relationship remains vital and that we are creating what we really want. Sixes represent responsibility, and it's up to us to assume responsibility in every aspect of our lives.

Seven is the number of reflection and refinement. The opposite of this reflective energy is the creation or presentation of obstacles, which are really signposts suggesting that it's time to turn our perception inward to explore and discover what is going on inside our own psyche. It's from within, and through acts of forgiveness and acceptance, that we refine our ways of relating and communicating. We also refine our values and our approach to our inner journey in life. Sevens represent spirituality as well, and spirituality must be a primary ingredient in every seven-governed relationship.

Much healing from past experiences can occur in these connections. They give us the opportunity to dive deeply into our selves and our lives, and to explore what could be different and what we want to change. And we will have the support energetically to make those changes realities, if we so choose. A spiritual path of some sort is necessary in a seven-based relationship, as without it there can be obstacles.

Eight represents power and abundance. Its energy is filled with command, determination, follow-through, and will. The energy of the number eight empowers us with the ability to make anything happen, and along with this ability comes the responsibility to integrity and right action. The eight displays the relationship between energy and intention, and in these relationships we will learn the art of directing energy through the use of our intention.

Being in an eight relationship brings forth the personal will in each person, and one of the things we have to watch out for and avoid is engaging in ego battles—pure will, head-to-head combat. Consequently, the learning that often takes place for individuals engaged in an eight relationship has to do with personal interaction and the preservation of clear boundaries while interacting with another through love, thought, and action. Much personal growth can be accomplished in an eight relationship if one is willing to be humble and observant. Once we are on the path of great self-awareness in these relationships, we can then turn our focus to our relationship with life and the power we have to co-create through the use of our intention. Eight-governed relationships can bring forth tremendous abundance through the right use of power.

Nine is a universal number, which means it's more impersonal than the others; it involves the individual or the relationship that it governs in the greater scope of humanity. Nine represents re-creation and reinvention, often through loss or letting go of someone or something. Experiences that come forth from the nine influences encourage us to release the past and be open to new ways of relating, thinking, and perceiving life in general. This is highly creative, spiritual energy that must be met with receptivity and responsiveness. In a relationship that is governed by a nine, there can numerous opportunities to let go of old emotional wounds, past experiences having to do with relationships, and old ways of seeing ourselves and our lives. The influences that reside in this number are very demanding in what they require of us.

Relationships governed by one of the nines are karmic relationships, and the learning opportunities can be constant; so when we are involved and engaged in these connections, it's important for us to be open, receptive, and responsive in the best ways possible. Most of us are changed in powerful and positive ways through these relationships, especially when we are open and honest with ourselves in regard to the greater laws of life. These are not always long-lasting connections; however, they are most certainly meant to be for whatever duration they are present in our lives. Often, people with whom we have a nine connection come and go throughout time.

Ten represents accomplishment. The dynamics in a ten relationship are strong and powerful. Both individuals are empowered to manifest more of their individual expressions in life. Individuals with a ten as a birth card seek success and find it. This energy is filled with driving ambition, often containing force and focus. The energy of ten is like an ace ten times over. In a ten relationship, there must be acknowledgement of one another's individuality and continued support for each other's ambitions and personal expression. Independence is key.

Being and sharing with others personally as partners, and professionally as individuals, is very important if we are to thrive as individuals within a ten relationship, and if the relationship itself is to thrive. With this composite, it's important to embrace the power of the relationship through the connection of your love for one another, as there can be a danger of becoming too individualized, which can lead to separation. Ten-governed relationships are great for working together as partners or for working with groups or foundations.

Jacks represent initiation. They are the gatekeepers into the royal kingdom. Jacks are creative, clever, and freedom loving. Depending on the suit, a jack relationship can be playful, aloof, or dynamic. Each one is distinctive and brings out the uniqueness of each individual in the relationship. These connections must have strong elements of adventure and creativity, whether the activities we choose are totally mundane or completely exciting and exotic. Striving for the highest values will bring us the greatest rewards, and integrity will always be a vital key for guaranteed success. If we remain open and receptive to change and new awareness, our perception of our self and our life can be greatly enhanced. The jack relationship does not easily tolerate a lot of drama or emotion. Such patterns are quickly brought to the surface to be recognized and released; any choice other than letting go of them will result in alienation and create taxing situations in the relationship.

Queens rule through their service to humanity. The Queen of Hearts rules through her compassion; the Queen of Clubs through her communication; the Queen of Diamonds through her commitment to values; and the Queen of Spades through her service and healing of humanity. The intelligence within each of the queens is powerful and perceptive. Their personalities can be moody and overly sensitive, so balance and harmony are very important for the environment of a queen relationship, as is clear communication. Queen-ruled relationships cultivate self-awareness relative to others, and personal participation with humanity through the acts of service.

In a queen-ruled relationship, we must honor and adore, in demonstrative ways, our partner, friend, child, or whomever we are in the relationship with. Self-recognition and recognition of one another are crucial. These connections awaken our perception and intuition in refined, eloquent ways. We must take care in these relationships not to become overly dramatic or take things personally when they have nothing to do with us. Nitpicking and self-absorption are signs that we are tuning into this energy at its most static frequency. The highest side of the queen is manifested through compassionate, intelligent, and wise service to others.

Kings are the masters of their respective suits. Kings are commanding and filled with power and presence. Kings like to be in charge, and they should be in command. However, balance must be kept so that command does not turn into control, forcefulness, or misuse of their inherent power. In a king-governed connection, the desire to be in command can spill over into the relationship. These relationships can be very empowering on the personal level, as long as each person supports the other, outwardly expresses recognition, and assumes responsibility for these things at the personal level. These relationships can bring great good fortune to those involved in them as a couple or as business partners. Respect is the magic key that opens the unlimited realms of these relationships.

The Fifty-Two Relationship Combinations

Love isn't a decision. It's a feeling. If we could decide who we loved it would be much simpler, but much less magical.

—Trey Parker and Matt Stone

At the end of each compatibility report, you will find "the Keys to the Kingdom" for each card, which outline the key elements that will unlock the highest blessings and greatest opportunities of each connection. The keys for each kingdom are the four most important ingredients the relationship must have to thrive, and they are unique for each of the composite cards. Surviving is not an option in a relationship. If you are merely surviving, you're either missing the point of the relationship or ignoring its gifts and remaining stuck in some past part of your emotional psyche. Or you may just be in the wrong relationship. When applied, the four keys will make your relationship all it can be, make it the best experience for you and your partner, and guide you on your journey to personal self-mastery.

The Relationship
Composite Cards

1
Ace of Hearts
The Desire for Love

Was this love at first sight, or did you have the feeling that you were throwing caution to the wind?

The Ace of Hearts represents the conception and birth of new life and new love. It represents new beginnings in relationships both with one's self and with others. Deep down, each of us is motivated by the desire to love and be loved, because this is human nature. The energy of this card is driven solely by that very desire, and with this innate longing come two questions: what can love do for me and what will love bring to me? Value plays a key role within this relationship connection. This ace must know the significance of any and all effort made in a relationship because the rewards gained will most definitely be measured along the way.

Aces by nature are selfish and driven by pure desire. This ace is no exception, and the characteristics of selfishness are likely to be brought forth in each of you as this relationship develops. Selfishness can be a positive or negative influence depending on how it's perceived. The independent energy of the Ace of Hearts can stir up uncertainty in regard to security, which comes from the insatiable need for love embodied in this card. This driving force of the Ace of Hearts is pure, raw, and intense, and it will be felt in your connection with one another. When this energy is focused outward into projects or global efforts, great change happens, and the results can be extremely rewarding for everyone. Remember that this card is the card of conception and brings forth new life.

This ace can lean toward being focused on being given to rather than giving at the personal level, and this tendency may show up for each of you exclusively. The secret language of a heart relationship says that giving is the key to having what is most valuable. Good self-esteem and a clear sense of self will pave the way for success, as will gratitude for what life is giving you. In fact, these elements are absolutely necessary for this partnership to work in the best possible ways and for each of you to feel secure within it. If these elements are not strong points for you, opportunities to grow in these ways will most certainly arise. When they do, it will be wise for you to take advantage of them in order to cultivate your relationship with yourself and with your partner.

Each of you will have a need for financial independence and control of your own money, and financial independence is what will work best in the partnership as well. Along with this connection comes an abundance of financial creativity, which can manifest for each of you as individuals and the two of you as partners. Often the desire for accomplishment can be taken to a global level rather than kept for personal needs, and both types of accomplishment are possible simultaneously. Working in the world together to make a difference can bring great good fortune.

Personal independence is a must with this connection. If you have a natural tendency toward codependency, if you tend to be needy in a relationship, or if you like your partner to depend on you, you are not likely to get what you think you need with this connection. However, this card's influence will bless you with great opportunities to successfully cultivate your independence. In addition, if you want someone to support your talents, ideals, and goals, and you want to do the same for a partner, this can be an amazing relationship.

In this relationship it's best to make a mental choice early on to expect the unexpected and the unusual. Things will always be changing in your life together, and flexibility will be the key to riding through these changes with ease. Old patterns will be revealed and put to the test, and if they are not useful in the present, they will be dissolved. Hopefully the dissolutions will happen by choice and with grace. This card represents the conception of life and love, new beginnings, and the birthing of the heart. Always embrace what is new, what is before you, and what is unknown, and you will develop your character in ways you didn't know were possible.

The Ace of Hearts influence will constantly create new situations that will lead you into your future, both personally and professionally. Joint goals and clear priorities will insure success in your togetherness. Romance is the key to passionate expressions of your self and your creativity. It's important to make your dreams the priority and keep your romantic life alive and juicy.

It is likely that you've called this relationship forth to strengthen your innate sense of self and your inner relationship with your self. An Ace of Hearts connection will give you many opportunities for character development and personal growth. The key that opens the doors to personal opportunity in this relationship lies in maintaining your independence and self-awareness as your first priority. The moment you become codependent, your connection with your partner will begin to decline. Working together toward related goals (with the goals as the focus rather than your partner) will establish a solid base of communication and trust between the two of you.

Exciting activities must be on the calendar regularly for your relationship to thrive. The more you explore and discover together, the better things will get. When you are on the move, you feel the power of this ace at work. Exploration and the discovery of new uncharted territories will deepen your bond of love and passion.

If you are presently in this relationship and experiencing challenges, think carefully over what is being said by the oracle and use this information to build a new foundation in your partnership. This connection is not for those who seek to depend on someone else to know their self. It's for those who have an independent spirit and enjoy coming face-to-face with the unknown. If you are not getting what you need in this relationship, look at it from a distance and see if it's really right for you. If you love this person in a healthy way and you could be more independent, grow yourself into being free of that which no longer serves you and step outside your comfort zone into a new freedom of self-expression. This is the opportunity that this card brings forth in connection with another person.

If you are considering entering this relationship, know that the dynamics described here will be the dominant energetic influences governing the partnership. If this sometimes-unpredictable, independence-based relationship sounds like it's not for you, you might want to look elsewhere for a companion. On the contrary, if you find the description of this relationship appealing, this relationship will give you an ongoing opportunity to grow by leaps and bounds, and you will learn to express yourself in new and exciting ways. You may also find yourself doing some very meaningful, life-changing work with others. Just be sure to follow the given guidance to insure real happiness.

The Keys to the Kingdom of the Ace of Hearts

Self-Esteem

Good self-esteem and the maintenance of your individuality are most important for each of you and for the two of you as a couple. Cultivate your individuality in artistic and creative ways. If you don't express it through your work, find an outside hobby that gives you a platform to express yourself in an independent way, as this will make you more attractive to your mate.

Exciting Escapades

Exciting activities and adventurous escapades insure a happy journey together. The Ace of Hearts loves whatever is new and not before seen, that which is untouched and unexplored. You must always feed this aspect of your relationship with wonderful explorations into the unknown—even if it's a journey to have breakfast on Sunday morning at a new bakery in the next town.

Giving Your Support

Give to your partner without the expectation of getting something in return. In this relationship, giving brings the greatest rewards. Support one another to be the individuals that you truly are. Support one another to be all that you can be. Know that the more you support your partner, the more support you will see coming your way, not just from him or her, but from outside sources as well. This magical formula must be employed to guarantee relationship success with this Ace of Hearts connection.

Shared Goals

While maintaining your personal goals and distinct self-expression, you must also have shared goals as a couple. Draw on your individual strengths and shared values to form your joint goals, and schedule time to work on them together. Then have an adventure together to celebrate them coming to fruition.

Note: These goals are best when they result in making a difference for someone else, such as doing volunteer work together, giving to a charity, or working for a cause. However, your goals can also be focused toward financial success and artistic expression. The ideal, of course, would be to do it all.

2
Two *of* Hearts

Union in Love

T he Two of Hearts represents union in love and the communication of the heart. However, the very things that make this
connection profoundly wonderful can also make it a bit of a
challenge at times, so the opportunities for learning are great and will
always be present throughout your time together.

Twos represent communication, cooperation, partnership, and
compassion. The positive side of this card is a delicious union of the
heart and the mind. This relationship can be like a dream come true
or a fairy tale. Communication, selfless giving, trust, and self-reflection
are the keys to the strength of this connection; when these strengths,
along with friendship and understanding, are brought forth in this
relationship, real love will be the result.

You may find, however, that there will be times when power struggles arise from each of you wanting to be in control and wanting to
have things your own way. These clashes will be the test. You will have
to guard against projecting blame onto your partner and thinking it is
he or she who has the problem and not you. At these times you must
remember that you are perfect mirrors for one another. Choosing to
make changes within yourself first will be the empowering and
supportive choice to make. Electing to do the opposite will be destructive to your relationship.

It's likely that you felt that you already knew one another before you
first met, and this could very well be the case, as this kind of relationship

is often one that is picking up from where it left off in another lifetime. Whether or not you believe in past lives, at the very least, this union has a powerful spiritual connection that cannot be denied.

One of the challenges that can present itself in this relationship comes in the form of each of you having unrealistic expectations of the other. This propensity may stem from having the same of your self. Take care when you are made aware that your expectations are unreasonable, as this type of behavior will lead directly to conflict. Also, be aware of the inclination to want to control your partner by thinking you know what's right and that he or she does not. These dynamics can play out in very subtle ways, and you must be honest with yourself about what you're communicating and what you are or are not projecting. If you find that you're rationalizing your behaviors, in those moments you are likely to be making up stories rather than owning the truth. This relationship connection will deteriorate with anything less than total integrity in communication.

Avoid getting stuck in ruts or routines, as doing so will quickly extinguish the fires of your passion. You and your partner will be happiest when you explore and discover new ways of being in relationship together.

The blessings that come with this connection are founded in love and communication. There can be tremendous generosity and desire to give to one another, which is really wonderful. Loving encouragement will create the most solid foundation for long-lasting love and happiness. Those times when you feel yourself faced with the need to control or confront, or when you see these needs in your partner, stop and turn the situation around by giving of yourself in a loving way. Friendship creates the building blocks for the foundation of this relationship.

It's likely that you have called this relationship to you to deepen your connection with yourself and to learn how to redefine your self-expression of who you are in an intimate relationship. The desire to connect deeply at the soul level is strong with this card, and the romantic expressions and loving devotion that live in this connection are rare and beautiful. Appreciation of what you have been given will nourish your relationship at its very roots. This is also a very fortunate card, so if you're inclined to work together, it could be very lucrative.

If you are presently in this relationship and experiencing the challenging aspects that this connection can evoke, which will show up as power struggles, know that these situations are opportunities to fine-tune your way of communicating—first with yourself and then with your partner. The person who stands before you is a mirror of your own relationship with yourself. Before projecting your fears or your need to be in control (which comes from fear) onto your partner, look first to yourself. Take a deep breath and tune more deeply into your own self-awareness and make the choice to cultivate who you really are. Then give yourself permission to give your love with kindness, free of fear. I guarantee you will be pleased with your decision to do so.

The Keys to the Kingdom of the Two of Hearts

Finely Tuned Communication

Keep it real, keep it honest, and keep it going, because this communication will be the very foundation that your relationship stands on. Sensitivity and integrity are musts in your verbal and nonverbal communication, as this card influence brings a delicate sensitivity and awareness of that which lies beneath the surface of what is being communicated. Secrets, lies, or withholding love will instantly destroy this relationship, and if this happens, you will have lost something ever so precious.

Selfless Acts of Giving

Giving to your partner, even when you think that you're not getting what you need, will play an essential role in establishing and maintaining trust between you. This relationship will teach you to go beyond your fears, and this lesson will be a major component of the learning that comes with this influence. Explore and discover new ways to give of yourself, and then do it. When the thought comes to give, take action.

The Commitment to Trust

This relationship can be plagued by old fears that are stirred up from past experiences. If this happens, you must heal those old wounds. Without a strong foundation of trust, this relationship doesn't have a leg to stand on. Fears will always be the greatest challenge with this connection, so go beyond them when they come up. Talking with your partner can help you do this.

Self-Reflection

Always remember that your partner is your mirror. When something comes up and you want to project it onto him or her, stop first and ask yourself, "How does this situation reflect how I am in relationship with myself?" Look inside your own emotions and beliefs, and be honest with yourself about what's really going on with your thinking and your emotions. This may be an area that needs extra attention through self-reflection. It will be worth your while to take the journey of letting go of your resistance and allowing your innocence to come forward in your personality.

3
Three of Hearts
The Creative Expressions of the Heart

Joy, love, and creativity are the essential expressions of the Three of Hearts. This relationship connection brings forth tremendous opportunities for greater understanding of one's self and one's emotions, and these are the personal arenas where a great deal of learning will occur for each of you regarding personal boundaries.

The Three of Hearts characterizes emotional creativity and embodies the longing for a love that satisfies the deepest part of our being. The challenge with this card as a relationship composite is that there can be a subtle, underlying uncertainty present in both parties. It will repeatedly show up in this relationship, as the Three of Hearts symbolizes indecision or uncertainty in love. Any number of expressions of this uncertainty can be present, including the "I don't want to lose what I have, but perhaps I should be somewhere else" syndrome, or the sense of "I love this person, but I don't feel secure." It is very likely that emotional drama will be a recurring event in this relationship. The energy of this card is fast moving and quick to change directions, which is part of what causes the feelings of doubt. Being active as individuals and as partners can alleviate the insecurities that are brought into play by the overactive mental-emotional qualities of this card. Communication also holds the power to subdue the sensations of doubt.

Good communication with one another and physical activities also are the secrets to creating mental balance and emotional harmony. You must have outlets for your creativity, talk on a regular basis, and have great physical intimacy for this to be a happy, drama-free experience. All of the aforementioned activities are natural expressions for the Three of Hearts, and it's just a matter of you and your partner engaging in them on a regular basis.

If you are in this relationship and you can relate to the uncertainty and indecision, you must know that these feelings will likely be present often and in subtle ways. It's only when you are engaged in communication or playing together in some way that they're not there. This relationship brings the opportunity to learn how to have a deeper, stronger connection with another in the most intimate ways. Each of you may need to learn and to choose to establish clearer personal and emotional boundaries. Your relationship will gain strength from the expression of affection and romantic gestures, deep communication, individual creative expression, and the constant re-creation and reinvention of your love connection. These are the things that will build the foundation of your relationship and nourish it as it grows. These things will also diffuse any doubt that arises.

If you are not yet in this relationship, but it's one you're considering, you must ask yourself if you want to be in a relationship where it's possible that you could often be feeling uncertain and unsure. If this potential partner is someone you love and enjoy being with, if you're comfortable being with him or her when there is no outside stimulation, and if you feel certain and secure when you are together, then there are other influences at work, and you can make your decisions based on what your experience is. Just be sure to be honest with yourself in regard to how you really feel, and choose to make the very best decision for yourself that you can. People who personally have the influence of the number three in their birth card love this energy and are right at home here. This can be a very beautiful connection of love and innocence, and it's important to acknowledge those qualities.

It could be that you have drawn this relationship to yourself because you want to learn to have better boundaries or because you want to be more expressive emotionally and creatively. Be aware and forthright in your first and primary relationship, which is the one you have with yourself, and make your choices with self-awareness.

Whether you are already in this relationship or you're being drawn to it through a potential partner, this type of connection says that you are seeking a deeper connection with your own soul. The attraction you have to this person is a call from deep within you to be in a more passionate relationship with your own self-expression, as well as in a more intimate relationship with another. When you bring your personal passion forward into this relationship, you will enjoy this connection and reap the fullest satisfaction that can be gained from it, which is a true expression of love and beauty.

The Keys to the Kingdom of the Three of Hearts

Articulating Creativity

You have the opportunity to support one another's creative aspirations, whatever they might be. And if they are buried, then you have the prospect of helping each other unearth those aspirations and bring them into unique expression. Finding comfort in being yourself and articulating your personal brand of authenticity will be a gift that is found with this connection over and over again.

Expressions of Affection

The importance of expressing physical and verbal affection cannot be stressed enough for this connection. These outward displays of love will eliminate any and all underlying feelings of uncertainty when they are present. Physical and verbal forms of love must be present on a consistent basis in order to establish and maintain emotional security and open communication between you and your partner.

Exploration and Adventure

Traveling and engaging in physical activities together will keep things alive and juicy and allow your intimacy to deepen more rapidly. Movement, adventure, variety, and change are experiences that feed this card's restless nature.

Personal Boundaries

In this relationship you will have the opportunity to learn to maintain clear emotional boundaries. Not doing so will create a back-and-forth, push-and-pull dynamic that will undermine the connection between you. Be true to yourself and your emotional needs, and honor the same for your partner.

4

Four *of* Hearts

Building Foundations of Love

The Four of Hearts symbolizes stability in love, family, and home, and it is one of the greatest cards to have governing a relationship. This card embodies a natural understanding of partnership and seeks to manifest this understanding with the highest possible values. The people in your lives will play important roles in your connection with one another, and love will be the very foundation that this relationship stands upon. *Stability* is the key word here, as this four indicates strength in both heart and mind. New learning and shared experiences highlight the connection between you, and communication is sought and shared with ease. Money and finances will be stable as well, and your work ethics will play an important role in the relationship.

The main challenge that can show up in this relationship has to do with getting stuck in routines or ruts, or in becoming too fixed in your own attitudes or ideas to be open and receptive to your partner's ideas and wishes. This is not likely to happen too often, as the relationship flourishes in love and harmony. If you do recognize stubborn attitudes or behaviors riding up between you, it's best to deal with them directly and immediately. This is a very blessed card for relationships, and it is often identified as the marriage card of the deck.

If you are looking for stability, certainty, and longevity, you may have found the right companion. With lovingkindness, true compassion, and deep wisdom as its foundation, this relationship has the potential to last for a lifetime. This relationship provides the stability and security for dreams to be built on. The dreams that you bring into reality in this relationship have the ability to last beyond your generation and into the ones that follow, creating an ongoing stream of goodness.

If you are currently in this relationship and you are experiencing difficulty, you might have to give more of yourself to the relationship than what you have been accustomed to in the past or in other relationships. Heart relationships teach us the importance of unconditional love and acceptance, and the power of selfless giving. The negative or unconscious aspects of the heart energy can make us selfish or self-absorbed. Often when we are in these states of mind, we don't recognize them and then we project our misery onto our spouse. You cannot be in this relationship without being open and receptive. It simply won't work. Stubbornness will not fly with this connection. It's all about love and understanding. If you find that you're being stifled in some way, give more and expect less and see what happens. The magic will be found in giving.

If you are considering this relationship as a new possibility for yourself, if it feels right to you, if you are being honest with yourself in regard to what you want, and if you feel great about yourself when you are with this person, absolutely by all means go for it, and enjoy the blessings that life is giving you by bringing the two of you together.

The Four of Hearts is one of the most stable influences you can find for a relationship, especially if relationship itself is your focus. Some people get into relationships wanting to be taken care of or wanting to take care of someone else. Another reason is for companionship. The third reason is for a relationship in which the relationship itself is the primary focus. This card's life path embodies any and all of those characteristics for both parties as a relationship card, so it's an ideal foundation on which to build a lasting partnership.

The Keys to the Kingdom of the Four of Hearts

Outward Expressions of Love

Love is the very heart and soul of this relationship, and the application and expression of love in any and all ways will get you everywhere. Sharing with each other and with family and friends is a valuable component for each of you and for the partnership. Giving to one another is especially important, and it is something you will want to engage in continuously. Have fun and be creative in your expressions of generosity by giving to your partner in every way that you can, and know that they will come back to you tenfold.

Kindness

Always be kind. You are in this relationship to express kindness and love and to learn unconditional acceptance and compassion. These opportunities are the greatest gifts of this relationship connection, and learning the lessons that this card offers will open your heart in ways you didn't know were possible.

Openness and Receptivity

It's all too easy with any four influence to become fixed or stuck in some way. It's imperative that you avoid getting stuck in attitudes or ideas that keep you from growing or that interfere with communication between you and your partner. Be open and receptive, and listen with your entire being. *Openness, curiosity,* and *receptivity* are key words for this relationship connection.

Honor Your Sanctuary

Your home is your sanctuary. Though you may each go out into the world and do your work there, you come home to rejuvenate, to be renewed, and to dive deeply into your intimate connection of love. Create your home to be an altar to your love, as all other endeavors will stand on the foundation of this one to become strong and successful.

Five of Hearts

The Ever-Changing Heart

When developed and channeled, the influence of the Five of Hearts has the potential to establish a sense of stability and security. If this energy is not utilized productively or expressed and brought into form in a creative way, uncertainty, doubt, and confusion will weave their way through the threads of your connection. As a composite card, the Five of Hearts has the potential to create a somewhat unstable emotional environment in a relationship. There can be underlying feelings of uncertainty, winding like a river beneath the surface of your relationship. The shifting emotional sand of this connection is spawned by the abundant creative energy inherent in this card.

The Five of Hearts is driven by strong desires and thrives on variety. This card wants all it can get—of everything it wishes! That being said, the desire for material objects and personal freedom can generate challenging issues in a relationship. Toys and things that delight the senses are absolutely necessary to offset boredom. The finer things in life are essential. Freedom is important, and socializing and having others around is a given. Friends and family are central, and children are likely to play a very special role in this partnership as well. If you don't have children or pets, you may find that one or both of you work with kids or animals in some way.

This card embodies natural business savvy, and when that business sense is applied in the relationship (working together), you can make a lot of money. However, you might want to have someone else manage your money for you. Finances can become a bit blurred with this influence; it's important to keep a close watch over your money, as spending can easily get out of hand unless one of you is really good at saving. Love, fun, play, and people will all be in order and accounted for. Money, however, may slip through your fingers without you knowing where it went, as there can be a tendency to live beyond your means with this influence. You will have to pay attention to this arena of finance, because money can become an area of stress in the relationship.

You might find yourselves seeking to establish balance between working and playing, as both will be very important. You are likely to be either totally focused on one or the other or be completely scattered, with your energy going in various directions. Music or other forms of enjoyable sounds, such as the flowing water of a fountain, can be powerful elements that bring balance and harmony into your environment.

If you are thinking about getting into this relationship, be sure that you are emotionally comfortable with the unknown, as this influence in the cards really does have an air of restlessness in regard to emotion. If you prefer feeling stable and having unwavering certainty, this relationship may not be ideal for you. It is for those who are comfortable feeling unfettered and those who appreciate their independence. You will need a strong, solid emotional base within yourself to feel confident in this connection. If you have that, it can be a great adventure that is laced with tons of fun and exciting adventures. If you feel that you have that solid emotional base within, but you really don't, that discrepancy will be revealed to you, as well, and can result in an opportunity for greater self-confidence.

This is a great relationship for making money, sales, wheeling and dealing in real estate, or just simply bargaining with people. If you are presently in this relationship, know that the more colorful you make it and the more romantic and playful you are with your partner, the better it will be. Travel, explore, and have parties! It was probably a Five of Hearts that coined the phrase, "Variety is the spice of life." That phrase sums up the Five of Hearts energy in a nutshell, and variety and the spice of life are what this relationship will need to keep it juicy and keep it thriving.

It's important to know that there are many more connections that happen in the individual life paths indicated by the cards. If you both have strong four or eight influences in your personal cards, those influences will bring more stability into your relationship. The Five of Hearts is an umbrella of energy that covers the overall composure of the connection that you have with each other. The influences that are present will always be present. It's just a matter of how you choose to engage with them. This can be a very loving, playful relationship.

The Keys to the Kingdom of the Five of Hearts

Balance and Equilibrium

Maintaining balance and equilibrium in your relationship will be of utmost importance—balance between work and play, balance between spending and saving, balance between the time spent alone and as a couple and the time shared with others, and balance between each of your personal emotional environments. Also important will be to find things of mutual interest and intentionally make time for those activities on a regular basis.

Work and Productivity

Work will bring stability and security to this love connection. Whether you work together or not won't matter, although working together can be very great and very lucrative. Remember that work, the construction of ideas and things, or the building of something solid will bring four-type energy into the relationship and stabilize its foundation.

Change and Variety

Fives represent change, and change and variety must be strong elements in your lives together. However you choose to create this in your lives is of little consequence, as long as you initiate new experiences, travel, and social activities that feed the need for excitement in this card influence. Travel, especially, is a powerful tool for strengthening your bond and for satisfying this card's need for new experiences.

Straight from the Heart

Communication must come from the heart, and clarity of intention must be built into the delivery. Take care to avoid being overbearing, which can be a tendency with this card. You must also steer clear of having overly high expectations of your partner. If your partner isn't meeting your expectations, lower them immediately and remember to be grateful for what you have with this person. Emotions can get out of hand with this card, so be clear and honest, and remember to give of yourself first, as giving will insure harmony and trust.

6

Six of Hearts

Balance and Harmony

This is the card of cosmic love, and, without a doubt, the two of you were meant to connect. This is a profound soul mate connection—one where you feel as if you have been with this person forever—and often this feeling is strongly present in those moments when you first meet. The heart is the ruler of this relationship, and it has a mission. When the heart energy is so strongly present in a connection, the mind and ego can react strongly, so know that a lot of issues are bound to come up in this relationship. Each of your personal preferences for being in control will rise to the heights of their fullest expression, and in these moments there will be opportunities for increasing self-awareness and for personal transformation.

You must take care to establish clear emotional boundaries, as there can be a tendency toward excessive compromise for the sake of harmony and peace. Repeatedly making compromises in this way will surely create underlying frustrations and possible resentment over time. The Six of Hearts represents the karmic law of love, and this ultimate law has to be adhered to; give from the heart, from beyond the personality, from beyond the ego, and from beyond concepts. Perhaps you called this relationship to yourself to learn more deeply what pure love is really about or to learn about commitment to partnership in a greater way.

Power struggles are bound to occur. Do your best to engage in physical activities together, such as work, travel, and the exploration of new places or things, as these activities will diffuse the energy that builds up and creates tension. This connection also supports the initiation of new ideas for the world to see and gain from; however, shared values are the very bottom line with this connection. If your values are not aligned, you are wasting your time with one another.

Speak to one another with kindness and compassion, understanding and love. Clear, honest, and forthright communication is the key to making this a successful relationship. Playing or working together will aid in taking the edge off of the tremendous power and fixed attitudes that can exist with this card.

Sixes bring forth reasons for making adjustments and compromises in order to create balance and harmony from chaos and disorder. It's important to keep the mind in check in this relationship. Otherwise you will always be in conflict or misunderstanding each other about one thing or another, and the fire of love and passion will be put out by conflict and struggle. There is a potential for this to be a highly workable relationship and one that has deep, long-lasting ties from the past into the future. It's just a matter of having really clear boundaries and communicating with clarity, kindness, and receptivity.

It can take a lot of attention and a lot of work to prevent this relationship from being explosive and full of power struggles. As long as things are kept light and free of ego, it can be a very empowering connection for both parties. There is, however, a mysterious combination of passion and will. Each of you will have to remain clear with your intentions to have success and happiness in this relationship.

If you have drawn this relationship your way, it could be that you want to temper the flames of your passion and to be in balance with the wisdom side of your will. This connection is not for everyone, so be true to your innermost discernment regarding how you feel when you are with this person, and to your intuitive knowledge of whether or not this is the best intimate relationship for you. If you are presently in this relationship and you are experiencing challenges, practice the advice that comes forth from the oracle and see if you can bring forth the higher aspects of this card to bear its fruits of love, beauty, harmony, and balance. This can also be a very fortunate connection for each of you as individuals and together as a couple.

The Keys to the Kingdom of the Six of Hearts

Clear Discernment

Be open, receptive, and discerning in your communication with your partner. This connection will demand that you give in and give way rather than choosing to react when you feel you're not being heard, seen, or, most importantly, understood. The question you have to ask yourself in those moments is, "Do I want to be right, or do I want to be loved?" It will all come down to a matter of honoring the intrinsic value of the connection you have with one another rather than giving way to the ego.

Taking Action

It can be all too easy to become complacent with this connection, expecting life to come to you rather than you going out to meet it halfway. You have to get up and out, and out and about, as this card influence has a natural tendency toward complacency. Plan trips, work on projects together, and explore new avenues for putting yourselves in the limelight in some way.

Give and Take

To be proactive in making any necessary adjustments in your way of living and relating, come together and make reasonable compromises. Complacency will not work with this connection, and it takes both of you making the effort to keep things alive and moving forward. If you don't make these efforts, you might become bored in the relationship.

Responsibility to Integrity

It's ever so important to be open, honest, real, and sincere in your communication with one another. This is a major responsibility for this connection, and one that has to be put at the top of the priority list. It is against the law of this card to be dishonest in any way whatsoever. Therefore, you and your partner must have values for this connection to work its special brand of magic.

Seven of Hearts

The Union of Heaven and Earth

When the composite card indicates a Seven of Hearts relationship, trust is not only the force that governs the connection between you, but it must also be the very foundation that the relationship is built upon.

The Seven of Hearts is the card of forgiveness, acceptance, and unconditional love. The groundwork of this relationship must be based on those qualities. Open communication is an absolute must, and nothing short of that will work here. If this isn't the type of intimacy that you're looking for, this is not the relationship for you. However, if you want a relationship that is based on trust and a deep and beautiful love, then perhaps you have found exactly what you want. The Seven of Hearts can be one of the most spiritual connections in the deck.

This relationship will enhance your appreciation for beauty. Music, the literary arts, spiritual pursuits, or anything that is finely tuned or carries sentimental values, such as family, will be important to both of you. These things will be vital for the cultivation of the relationship as well. It's likely that it was a family gathering or event with friends that brought the two of you together initially. Your personal appreciation for the fineness of life will either be enhanced or challenged in this relationship.

This connection will bring forth opportunities to let go of underlying fears and old emotional wounds, usually related to abandonment.

When such experiences arise, you must face them and release them in order for your relationship to thrive. This card teaches us forgiveness, and if there are people in your past that you need to forgive, doing so will be the best choice to make.

Your home together will be your safe haven, and quiet time together will nurture the roots of your connection. Home, quality time in a refined environment, and new experiences of how to share your fears and feelings are the things that will take you to the deeper realms of intimacy. Jealousy and suspicion, which can come up with this connection, are best left outside the door of this partnership, as they will only undermine and deteriorate its foundation.

Within this composite there is an influence that can create frequent changes regarding what will capture and hold your interest; therefore, the need for variety will be high on the priority list. In addition to the many changes that will occur, life will continuously expand your horizons with new experiences and new learning. Be open to the unknown and optimistic toward new possibilities, as resistance or fixed attitudes will create separation and missed opportunities.

If you are already in this relationship, it's critical that you create a temple for your love. That temple must be built with trust and honesty and filled with beauty and kindness. Make time to be alone and go deep together. Have fresh experiences together. Let home be a sacred place where you grow yourselves and your relationship with intention and conscious awareness as you let go of old emotional fears and insecurities about being abandoned. It's okay to be afraid and be vulnerable with your partner. Give yourself permission to be free and unencumbered by the past; spread your wings wide to a new future and a new way of being that is a fuller expression of who you really are deep inside. This relationship has the power to bring forth that part of yourselves that perhaps you had been afraid to show to another. Take advantage of the gift of this relationship, even if it takes you outside what is comfortable for you.

The Seven of Hearts symbolizes spiritual love. Bring this element, in its purest expression, into your lives as the foundation for your existence together. How do you do that? The answer is through respect, kindness, and the recognition that each moment you have together is a precious gift and an opportunity to be vulnerable. The more present you are in those moments, the greater your rewards will be. This relationship is all about the heart in its purest form.

If you are considering this relationship, *feel* as you read what is being said here. This relationship is a journey of healing and spiritual growth. It's a voyage into new and uncharted territory within yourself—one where the past can be left behind and a new level of trust can be established in the very core of your being. You simply have to be clear that you are ready to take this journey, as it is a very special one indeed. If you are in this relationship, it can challenge you regarding any trust issues you might have. Be inventive and creative in allowing yourself to go beyond the ego and fear, and give yourself permission to step onto the platform of trust and see what happens.

The Keys to the Kingdom of the Seven of Hearts

Trust and Vulnerability

Feeling safe while exposing your vulnerability is the most profound facet of this connection. Let go of your fears of being left, and allow yourself to be loved deeply and completely, because without this deep sense of trust, discomfort and uncertainty will take you over. Trust your feelings, trust your partner, and trust the love that you feel as you follow your feelings into the purest realms of your essence.

Forgiveness

This card is the teacher of forgiveness. It takes courage to forgive. Forgive the past and yourself, if necessary, and open your heart to the embrace of this lovely healing energy, which embodies truth and beauty. The energy of the Seven of Hearts is an awesome influence in our lives. When this relationship comes your way, you are truly being blessed with the deepest kindness that life has to give, and you will learn to have compassion for yourself and others in ways you have not known before.

Truth and Beauty

Surround yourself with beauty in all ways, at all times. This card represents beauty at its finest, and its energy will refine you and your life in every way if you allow it. All you have to do is pay attention and allow the grace of this card's influence to move through you and around you.

Acceptance

Acceptance is a major teaching of this card's influence. Because it is the card of spiritual love, it brings forth opportunities, through experiences with others, for us to learn to accept, forgive, and love unconditionally. Opportunities will arise for you through different situations that present themselves, and you'll have the chance to choose the higher aspects of this card. Remain aware and choose wisely.

8
Eight *of* Hearts
The Power of Love

The Eight of Hearts represents the transformational power of love and reveals love's magic in tangible ways through its expressions of beauty. With this power comes the responsibility to use love wisely and with care, because this card also embodies the power of persuasion. The influence of this card in a relationship is characterized by the expression of love that you share through your acts of giving to one another. Sharing your heart freely will generate the fuel that feeds the fires of love and passion, and it is what will keep them burning throughout time.

The Eight of Hearts emanates a persuasive magnetic charm, which will be expressed throughout your relationship with one another and perceived by those around you. This relationship can actually be quite magical. It's possible that you'll find yourselves surrounded by people who love and admire the two of you and marvel at your relationship. For this reason, it's vital that you keep a clear head about yourselves, as all of this attention has the potential to create a touch of delusion in the relationship. If you don't stay on top of your mind (meaning, if you aren't mentally disciplined), your fantasies could undermine the foundation of your connection with one another. Clear, practical—*practical* being the operative word here—communication is necessary and must take place on a consistent basis. Without it, you might find yourself waking up from a dream turned nightmare. So it's imperative that you stay present and be realistic.

Be generous with one another. Do practical activities together. Travel over the seas and spend time near the water.

You will have opportunities to heal your past in this relationship. Please take advantage of these times and do the work, as in doing so you will strengthen your bond of love and deepen your communication and connection. This relationship has its own brand of fantasy going on, and it can be a very delicious journey for a couple. Although it may be necessary to pull your heads out of the clouds from time to time and take note of where you actually are and what is really going on around you, it is a very blessed connection indeed.

If you are presently in this relationship, you have the opportunity to learn about communication in deeper and more practical ways than ever before, so take advantage of them. Being in love and having integrity are the keys to this relationship thriving. The eight-governed connection can cause the personal will to be strong, so it's imperative to be open and receptive and supportive of your partner's needs and his or her personal expression of self. There will be power struggles if you let your fear or your ego get in the way. Generosity is the key that unlocks the door to true love in all heart relationships and in this one in particular. When you give selflessly, you are taken out of your old unconscious patterns and into a new way of being in relationship.

If you are not yet in this relationship but are considering it as a possibility, keep a clear head as you enjoy the magnetic charm and heartfelt magic that you feel when you are with your partner. These are very real energies that are present for you to engage in and enjoy. Maintaining a sense of practicality will keep this connection grounded in reality. This can be a very lovely, long-lasting, extremely empowering relationship.

The Keys to the Kingdom of the Eight of Hearts

The Generosity of Love

The true power of this connection is pure love. When I say *pure,* I mean pure. There is great magic in this connection, and the magic must be honored with self-awareness if you are to reap its greatest benefits. Choose to ride high on the magic carpet of love by giving of yourself. Express your true generosity to your partner and to others. Share the wealth of your love so that the entire world can see and gain from it, and you will be greatly rewarded. If you choose another way of being in this relationship, such as from your ego or a desire to be in control, you will miss the benefits and destroy the gifts this relationship brings. Love with all of your heart, and watch the magic unfold before your eyes.

Fantasy versus Reality

Your communication with one another must be grounded in the practical world of the mundane. It's all too easy to get lost in the fantasies of love with this card, so in your thinking, your actions, and your decisions, you must help one another to stay focused and grounded in that which is sure and solid. Balance your fantasies with reality, and all will be well.

The Right Use of Charm

Responsibility to your integrity is an absolute must with this connection. Your charm and grace will be exalted with this card, and you must take care to use these gifts of love with the highest integrity and conscious awareness. With this card influence comes a power to manipulate. Avoid the temptation to misuse the magical powers that are bestowed by this card by choosing to act with integrity by taking responsibility in your thoughts, words, and actions.

Extraordinary Adventures

New discoveries are important. Spend time traveling to foreign places or uncharted territories that are close to home. The element of water is a strong influence for this relationship, so it's important to have water near or in your environment. It is also suggested that you travel over or on the water from time to time. Meeting new people, discovering new places, and finding new things together, especially away from home, will nourish each of you as individuals and, at the same time, strengthen the foundation of your relationship in practical ways. There is a risk of becoming lost in the world that you create for yourselves—hence the need for exploring and interacting with others.

9

Nine of Hearts

The Lessons of Love

The Nine of Hearts represents universal love and symbolizes love for all of humanity rather than one person. It's also known as the wish card, and perhaps this relationship appears to be the answer to a wish that you have or had. Please notice I used the word *appears,* as things are not always as they seem when this card is ruling a relationship. It's quite possible that the two of you met at a function that had to do with a greater purpose or cause for humanity, some sort of meaningful gathering of like-minded people, or just a gathering of people in general.

When this card shows up, it guarantees that there are valuable lessons to be learned, and bumping into disappointment, which can result from values that are not clearly defined, is mostly how these opportunities for learning will emerge. The Nine of Hearts connection offers you and your partner windows into the past that will reveal old patterns needing attention and transformation through the awakening of your awareness and through emotional healing. This card focuses on completion of the past—of situations from this lifetime or previous ones, depending on your beliefs, experiences, and reality itself. Your partner may be someone you've been very close to in another lifetime, and your encounter is an opportunity to connect and possibly complete your previous relationship. You have to pay attention to how things unfold. Obstacles will show up if you try to hold onto a fantasy about what you think this relationship should be;

they will also surface when you hold onto the past and are unwilling to let go of what is no longer serving you or the relationship. Opportunities to let go and open up to new learning are guaranteed to present themselves with this card governing your connection.

The Nine of Hearts corresponds to learning lessons about one's self through relationships, and these lessons come up often within this connection. It's not the easiest life path for a partnership, unless you are willing to be a student of life and adopt the highest of values in conjunction with a new way of being and thinking in regard to relationship. Your inner mental and emotional worlds will be mirrored big time through your interactions with your partner. So when issues come up for you personally, remember that you are being asked to let go of something. The way to do that is to first look within yourself to find the root cause of the issues, or to see how these experiences are mirroring how you are in relationship with yourself. Once you clarify that, then sort through your thoughts and clarify what it really is that you want to communicate with your partner. Being clear with your own mind first, and then your real intentions regarding your relationship, will prevent you from projecting your issues onto him or her.

Choosing to focus on global causes and issues as a couple can be a great thread that brings the two of you closer, as can giving to others to improve the quality of their lives. Because this card represents universal love and letting go, you must always look at yourself first to see what's going on with your own emotions. Then you can communicate with your partner from the understanding that you gain through your introspection and reflection. The real secret of the Nine of Hearts is to view your life from an impersonal point of view to attain a greater perspective of what's really going on.

All of the nines in the deck are thought of as universal cards, and when you have a life path governed by nine, be it a personal path or a relationship path, you or it belongs to the universe, making it more impersonal. Nines also symbolize loss, regeneration, and new beginnings that emerge from endings. On the high side of things, once you learn to let go and discover the natural rhythms of this energy, great goodness and love will come into play. The secret is to open your heart, your mind, and your life to a greater understanding of self and life, and to also allow yourself to touch your own innocence. When you do, there will be wonderful rewards for you as an individual and for your relationship.

An abundance of benevolence will manifest with this connection, and it will be most important to become attuned to, embrace, and cultivate this goodness on a daily basis. This is actually a very sweet connection. The heart suit represents love; though the energy of this card can seem tough at times, if you take the time to be aware of how you approach your partner with your communication, and if you are disciplined with your emotions, you can have a beautiful experience of uniting in love.

If you are presently in this relationship, it would be wise for you and your partner to find a global interest or cause that you want to support. Watch for stubborn behaviors in yourself and your partner, and step back to observe how destructive resistance can be. If this behavior is yours, change it! Selfless giving is the key to making this connection a happy experience, so give rather than expecting to receive. Expectations will lead directly to disappointment. Generosity with your affection will immediately ignite the magic, and your relationship will ride on the wings of pure love.

If you are thinking about getting into this relationship, be wise and be sure before proceeding. Take your time exploring how you feel when you're together. Be realistic in your observations and your evaluation of the connection that you have together, rather than projecting your fantasies onto the situation. This connection is for those who want to grow emotionally and spiritually, and for those who are willing to sacrifice themselves in the name of the relationship. If this is you, then go for it. If not, perhaps you would be happier in another relationship altogether. However, either way, it's important to honor the fact that this person has shown up for a reason and in reality the learning has already begun. For the best outcome, the direction of the relationship is best left in the hands of the gods.

The Keys to the Kingdom of the Nine of Hearts

Selfless Offerings

Giving of yourself without expecting to get something in return is the master key in this connection. This type of expression of the heart is so important that it cannot be stressed enough. Openness to receiving is also important. The law of the land in a Nine of Hearts relationship says that giving must be impersonal. So as individuals and as a couple, you must give first to each other and then to others, in both cases with the pure intention of enhancing the quality of life.

Authenticity

You must be authentic and honest, and you must always have integrity in your words and actions, because when you choose otherwise, your actions will come back to you in ways that are uncomfortable and disconcerting. A foundation of integrity is vital for this connection.

Work Together

Work together to make the world a better place, as this kind of work will become the glue that bonds your connection. If working together is not of interest to you, then perhaps a shared belief system, spiritual practice, or some sort of mental discipline will suit you. There does need to be some sort of shared experience of self-cultivation for this connection to thrive.

Gratitude

Recognize the gift of love that comes with this relationship, embrace it with all of your being, and you will be happy. The expression of your gratitude will play an important role in your ability to love one another. You can't take this love for granted, because if you do, it will actually work against you. That's the lesson of the Nine of Hearts. Know when to give, and know when to let go—and cultivate this rhythm, as this is the secret to success for this relationship. Pay attention. Cultivate your awareness continuously, and become more and more self-aware. Choose to be gracious in your interactions. It's all too easy for old, unconscious patterns to emerge with this card, so stay alert and be responsive to what you know is right thought and action.

10
Ten of Hearts

Idealism in Love

T he Ten of Hearts represents idealism in both love and leadership. This card embodies power-packed heart energy and lots of it. The characteristics personified by this card not only manifest in the personal realms of life, but also reach out to embrace community.

The Ten of Hearts path is one of good fortune and great love. The request from life is that you work hard for what you want, as hard work is an expression of gratitude for what you are going to be given as a result of your effort. The Ten of Hearts is a magical influence that grants wishes to those who believe they can have what they truly want.

Personal power and individuality are strong ruling elements in this relationship. Passion, optimism, and a sincere heart are the driving forces that keep things real and deep between you. Love is renewed on a regular basis and is the very fuel that feeds the engine of this connection. Romance is a key factor for your self-expression. Higher values are a must, as there can be a tendency for this card to be excessively concerned with material gain, which is fine, as long as integrity and right action are kept intact. If motives are askew, they must be examined and brought into alignment with the understanding of higher values.

This connection creates a fondness for playfulness, socializing, and entertaining. Much good fortune can come from gathering with others, whatever the event may be. The two of you will draw people your way, and you are likely to be admired by friends and family. This is a very happy relationship connection.

Jupiter, the strongest ruling influence for the Ten of Hearts, is the planet of expanse and good fortune, so there will certainly be an abundance of goodness in its many forms. You will be drawn to, and you will draw to you, people of influence, intelligence, and interest. This card suggests that you get out and be social, while exercising the inquisitive aspects of your nature; if you don't do this, you risk becoming bored, which can lead to a loss of interest in life and the relationship.

Honesty is a must, and it is the key to success with this connection. If honesty is missing in your communication or behaviors, disappointment will come knocking on the door, and things will deteriorate—rapidly. Hidden agendas, keeping secrets, or telling lies will rip the fabric of this connection, to its destruction. Forthrightness is the true way of the Ten of Hearts.

Being with kids or youths can be wonderfully stimulating and highly rewarding for both of you and for them. Service of some kind to humanity will bring great rewards as well.

If you are presently in this relationship, keep things alive and juicy by going out together, traveling, entertaining, and socializing with friends and family. Go dancing, take weekend trips to neighboring towns—do things together for the sake of being together. Find ways to give to your community. You must have fun being together for this to be a healthy connection. Keep things light, as heavy stuff will not fly in this relationship at all. This heart is full.

If you are considering this relationship for yourself, know that it can be great fun! If you want a complacent experience of living, however, this may not be the right place for you. You can and will enjoy the simple joys of being together at home, but if your partner wants more action in the relationship, you must respond, or he or she will become bored. You can easily live a normal existence, but you also have to engage in outside activities on a fairly consistent basis to keep things juicy, alive, and healthy. A relationship with this composite has the potential to be very, very great!

The Keys to the Kingdom of the Ten of Hearts

Socializing

Create a great social life for yourselves, and make time to be with friends and family. These types of activities will nourish your connection and bring joy to you and those you interact with. Great good fortune can show up when you are gathered with others, so welcome invitations with optimism and receptivity.

Community Involvement

Participate together in projects that enhance the lives of those less fortunate—especially kids. This connection will naturally inspire you to do so, and when you act upon this inspiration, you will become leaders of others via your inspired motivation.

Shared Interests

Shared interests are a must for each of you to feel fed by your connection. You are together to love and inspire one another, so let that happen. All doorways must be opened. Let the curiosity of this card open your mind to new things and open your mouth to openly share your experiences, so that you actively excite one another in the most authentic and delicious ways.

Honesty

You must be honest at all times in this relationship. If you have any hidden agendas, they will smack you right in the face. No hidden agendas, no lies, no secrets. Your strongest foundation will be built on openness, honesty, vulnerability, and receptivity.

11

Jack of Hearts

The Devotion of the Heart

The Jack of Hearts is the card of sacrificial love, and it represents the path of forgiveness, love, and compassion. In this relationship, all matters of the heart must be taken impersonally; if not, heartache and disappointment will be the result. That can be a very challenging dynamic to live with in an intimate relationship, unless you are committed to a path of self-mastery or spiritual growth. I'm not saying that this is a bad relationship or that it's doomed; however, it can have its rough spots, and knowing where they are and how to navigate them will be helpful for both of you.

It could be that you were drawn to this relationship to learn greater emotional and mental discipline, and there was probably something a bit unusual in the air when you first met.

The two of you will have to reinvent and recreate who you are, what you are doing, how you interact with one another, and what your lives are all about many times over. This relationship demands that you let go of old habits or patterns that no longer serve you. It's about healing past hurts and wounds, and moving forward with forgiveness and a new understanding of love and self. It's about learning to forgive and trust, and there can be underlying feelings of self-sacrifice that live within the unconscious body of this partnership. If you experience these types of feelings, it's a sign that these are areas within yourselves where work can be done to heal the past and free you to be more fully in the present. Your opportunity in this relationship is to look for the hidden gifts that reside in the challenges that arise and, like an alchemist, turn the challenges into opportunities for self-learning and personal growth.

The Jack of Hearts can be a master of denial. When things don't go the way you want them to or the way you expect them to, in that moment you have an opportunity to *let go* of your expectations and open your eyes to see the greater opportunity that life is offering in the moment, because there is always going to be one. It will be impossible to see the learning opportunities before letting go of your expectations, which function as blinders to the truth. When you find that you are feeling or experiencing resistance, stop, feel, listen, and turn within. Let go. Move forward. Breathe. Accept. Choosing these actions will open the doors to your greatest opportunities.

This relationship is a personal initiation for each of you. It's an initiation into the higher aspects and awareness of the heart and of love, and into a greater understanding of kindness and compassion. If you aren't able to see these opportunities when they show up, this relationship will be a difficult journey of miscommunication and misunderstandings, which will lead to the downfall of the relationship and whatever else is connected to it. The learning that exists here has to do with personal emotional boundaries.

Flexibility is a key word for this partnership, and you will have many chances to practice this. To be in a Jack of Hearts relationship is to become like the willow tree—you must bend. Clear personal boundaries have to be learned and set, as giving too much will later create resentment. Sacrifice will also lead to resentment; giving from the heart will lead to joy. Understanding the distinct difference between giving and sacrifice is a major lesson for this card. You are not in this partnership to be a martyr; that is the consciousness of a victim. You will have numerous opportunities to learn this lesson and grow in your ability to maintain emotional balance and establish clear personal boundaries.

Engaging in some sort of work will have the most grounding effect for each of you personally. Work, work, work—this is extremely important with this connection. Be productive as individuals and as partners, and work diligently to accomplish whatever goals you have set for yourself and for your partnership. These actions will stabilize your connection and bring the success you truly desire.

This relationship card is very profound—for better or worse—and its influences will not change. However, you can choose to engage in ways that will bring out the highest side of this most loving and gifted influence in the cards.

If you are in this relationship, it may be helpful to know that this is a path of love, forgiveness, and diligence. This card of sacrificial love is a highly spiritual influence; it's a card of initiation. It's not an easy relationship path unless you understand the true message that it carries, which is to become selfless in your giving while learning to establish and maintain clear emotional boundaries. This is not always the easiest thing to do, but it is an amazingly rewarding accomplishment when you do it. The results you create in your relationship will be based on the choices you make moment by moment.

If you are thinking about entering this relationship, know that the influences spoken of here will be present for the duration of your time together. Remember, the influences don't change. You, however, can choose how you communicate and interact within yourself and with your partner, and those choices will determine your outcomes. Perhaps you have called this relationship to yourself to learn and grow in new ways. Like the alchemist, you will become a teacher of love from what you learn in this partnership, because the high side of the Jack of Hearts is the one who shows the way of love. It's a very profound card. When this connection is manifesting in its purely positive energy, you will experience the power of love and the goodness it brings into your world. Look deeply and reflect with care to be aware of how you really feel in relationship with this person. Be honest with yourself.

The Keys to the Kingdom of the Jack of Hearts

Personal Boundaries

If you don't already have them, you must learn to create strong personal and emotional boundaries. You will do this by maintaining equilibrium between your acts of giving and receiving. Sacrifice is not giving. Learning the difference between the two will be a major lesson within this relationship.

Balance and Poise

The challenges that this card presents will be brought into balance through physical activity and acts of productivity. It's important to avoid overindulgence with things that appeal to the senses. Indulgence is fine, but overindulgence can lead to personal downfalls. Pleasure can be a great outlet for the abundance of energy that comes with this influence and a good way to escape dealing with deeper emotional issues that are bound to arise. However, if not kept in check, overdoing anything can be destructive and become an avenue for escapism.

Truthfulness

Being truthful is the key in your communication with one another. There may be a tendency to be otherwise, which will not work. You must possess a commitment to honesty and integrity for this relationship to grow into the strong bond of love that it has the potential to be. This is a card of love, trust, and innocence, and when these qualities are embraced and sustained by you and your partner, they create experiences of love that are awesome and empowering.

Embracing the Present

Let go of the past and embrace the present. If disappointments or frustrations arise, they are opportunities for you to learn how not to project your expectations onto your partner. In these moments it will be advantageous to observe your feelings, embrace the moment, and move forward to find clarity and resolution inside your own mind. Letting go of expectations and old stories will allow happiness to manifest freely in your relationship. Intend to be in the present and in the moment.

12
Queen of Hearts
The Fires of Beauty and Passion

The Queen of Hearts is a card of beauty, magnetism, affection, and idealism. She is the queen of love and compassion. The sensitive, receptive energy of this card naturally supports love and marriage, which makes it a wonderful influence for a relationship. Romance, home, family, and friends will be highlighted. This connection can feel like a fairy tale or a dream come true.

A fondness for comfort and fine living will saturate the fabric of this relationship, and money will likely find its way to you with ease. It's imperative that you appreciate the good fortune that comes your way, rather than taking things for granted. Practice gratitude for what you have and gratitude for one another, and the power of this queen's magic will make your dreams come true.

Known as the mother of compassion, the Queen of Hearts embodies and emanates unconditional love. A relationship that is under her rule has within it a responsibility to the higher expressions of love and kindness. Being in this relationship will require your attention and your self-awareness in this regard, and it will also reveal to you the places within yourself where compassion is not yet the priority. This queen opens our hearts to the universal powers of love and compassion, and when governing a relationship, she can bring unlimited blessings of love and joy.

On the more shadowy side of the Queen of Hearts lies a danger of becoming either overly self-absorbed or preoccupied with drama and emotions, or even preoccupied with the good fortune that comes with her blessings. For some, this connection can evoke the risk of addiction or overindulgence of some kind; if addiction is part of your or your partner's history, these types of behaviors will have to be watched closely if you want to have a healthy relationship. Overindulgence in unhealthy behaviors will create severe mental imbalances that lead to intense emotional drama in the relationship. Power struggles can also be a challenge with this connection and must be kept in check. This is an extremely passion-filled influence, and you must take care to maintain realistic perspectives regarding yourselves and each other. Having clear, down-to-earth goals and realistic perspectives of one another will help both of you to remain clear and grounded and will give the relationship a solid foundation upon which to stand and grow.

Queens, in general, like to be in control, and control issues and willful battles will surely show up if egos are not kept in check. Remember that love is the key that unlocks all doors for the two of you. Love is your secret gift. Love is your power. Compassion and understanding are your rewards. This queen loves to indulge in fantasy, so keeping things real and practical is the key to your success and happiness.

If you are in this relationship, you have been blessed with a wonderful gift of love and sensuality, and these very attributes must be kept alive for your relationship to continue to thrive. Sharing what the two of you have with the world around you will bring even greater abundance. Exploring the depths of love together will keep your relationship alive and healthy, as will exploring the world together. Shared creative endeavors are a great way to fuel the fires of passion. If you are in this relationship and it is stormy and unpredictable, use the advice given here to calm things down and take your connection with each other to its fullest potential.

If you are considering this relationship, be consciously aware and have a wonderful time. The call of love is at your door and waiting for you to answer. Be open, receptive, and most of all, realistic. There is a lot of illusion here that can sweep you away into fantasy if you are not paying attention, so keep both eyes wide open. Love, romance, and everything delicious are waiting for you to partake of them. Just know that you must keep emotions and ego in check, and stay balanced and centered within yourself to reap the greatest rewards of this queen's glorious gifts.

The Keys to the Kingdom of the Queen of Hearts

Tangible Expressions of Love

Love is the keeper of the magic for this connection. It will be easy to express your love and kindness to each other, as your emotional sensitivity will be heightened with this connection. Affection is important; touching, saying kind words, and giving little gifts now and then will spark the fires of this queen's sensual nature, and these types of actions will be very important for the longevity of the relationship. Remain aware and let your hearts shine for the world to see.

Compassion

You have the opportunity to learn true compassion and share it with the world. Your Queen of Hearts relationship embodies the wisdom of love and compassion that emerges from kindness and selfless giving. Find ways to share your understanding of this wisdom with the world through volunteer work of some kind. This type of work will keep you realistic in your personal perspectives and in the choices that you make as individuals and as a couple.

Curiosity in Love

Explore more deeply who you are as individuals. Explore each other with curiosity and receptivity. Explore the world around you separately and together. Be like children in your sharing of your discoveries and finds, and encourage one another to be the individuals that you truly are. Allow yourselves to resonate with the unique personal characteristics that will emerge from within you in the presence of this queen's influence.

Self-Awareness

The potential for power struggles is lurking in the lower realms of the kingdom of this relationship, and you must be careful that you avoid these types of behaviors. Every card influence has conscious and unconscious traits and expressions. Remember that with this queen on the throne, self-indulgence will lead straight to emotional chaos and misery. Cultivate your self-awareness and make choices that keep you in the throne of love, rather than in the dungeon of despair.

13

King of Hearts

The Exalted Heart

Yummy is a good word for this connection. Without a doubt, this can be one of the juiciest connections in the deck. There's no doubt that magic was in the air when this union was formed. This connection is sensual and emotional, and it was destined to be. The King of Hearts is the master of love and beauty, and this connection can bring about very deep and powerful expressions of love. It can be an evocative sexual connection as well. This relationship will have a strong element of emotional drama to it, so the use of sound logic will be critical in your communication with one another.

Imperative in this relationship is each of you making the choice to process your emotional challenges through your logical mind before expressing your feelings to your partner. The danger in not doing so is that your emotions could flare out of proportion, creating conceptual projections that will ignite chaos between you and in the relationship. Logic and common sense in both your thinking and your communication will keep your personal expectations of each other in the realm of the realistic. Use your intelligence and your reasoning to process your emotions by thinking them through first, so that you have clarity and mental stability when you express what's on your mind. The King of Hearts' energy is highly dramatic, emotionally fueled, and passionate. But, as juicy as it can be, it can also be a wild ride of drama if emotions override intelligence.

Deep in the belly of this powerful, loving king lies fear. The fear is accompanied by an innate tendency toward self-criticism. If you personally have these types of issues going on with yourself, they will come rushing to the surface of your conscious mind and into the relationship. The best thing you can do is deal with them independently in a masterful, kingly, mature way, rather than propel them into the relationship where they will damage the fabric of its very core.

The lessons that come with this card's life path have to do with mastery over the fear of rejection. The journey goes from emotional immaturity to the expression of compassion and understanding for one's self, as well as an enhanced global awareness of life. This journey will be part of your relationship, and it's a worthwhile passage indeed. Past fears and self-editing will not work here, so it's best to discharge them to another place and time by recognizing where they came from and where they actually belong.

Selfishness, especially with personal time, can be an issue with this connection, as can being consumed in self-gratification or overindulgence. If your personality leans in either of those directions, you might want to pay closer attention to these tendencies and stay on top of them so they don't create separation in the relationship. The higher side of this connection is all about love and beauty. Whatever issues you have from the past, facing and clearing them will be well worth the effort. The result will be the royal gift from this gracious, loving king and from the true relationship he has bestowed upon you—knowledge of the true magic of the heart.

Every king-governed relationship has to do with learning self-mastery of some kind. The King of Hearts rules over the emotions and the manifestation of love and beauty through the expression of compassion and grace. One reason you may have called this relationship to yourself is to learn how to become more masterful with your emotions and to be more open and receptive to being in a deeply intimate experience with another. Another reason for bringing this relationship into your life would be to allow yourself the gift of being blessed with a delicious love that is filled with beauty and harmony. The secret to making this a wonderful relationship is your commitment to becoming more aware of the true ways of the heart. Without this type of personal intention, communication will be blinded and one-sided, and the relationship will spiral downward into confusion and then fear, leading straight to emotional separation.

Openness and receptivity—both verbal and nonverbal—are musts, and the responsibility must be to integrity. Aligning with the king's power will enhance your personal skills and abilities, and put you in touch with the greatest expressions of your innate gifts of creative intelligence. This king's influence will also refine and enhance your intuitive intelligence as well. If you have a dream that has been sitting on the shelf, it's likely that being in this relationship will steer your dream to become a reality; all it will need is your permission.

The Keys to the Kingdom of the King of Hearts

Balanced Emotions

Outdoor activities and time spent in nature are a very important way of keeping balanced emotions between the two of you. You must support one another's individuality and creative expression, and give each other the space to *be* as well. Emotional balance is established from mental stability. Both must be sought in this relationship, as there can be a tendency toward overindulgence. Overindulgence can also lead to poor physical health in this relationship. It's imperative to keep desires in check. When desires are not kept in balance, emotions will become chaotic, giving way to underlying fears that take you on a roller-coaster ride of miscommunication, and on into anger and confusion. Fears must be realistically addressed, put in perspective, and transformed into trust.

Trust

The great opportunities of this relationship involve learning to trust more deeply, and it's important that you consciously choose to practice trust with one another. Listen to the beat of your heart rather than the fear and insecurity created by your mind. Yield rather than dominate, as domination stems from unacknowledged fear.

Choosing to Be Present

When communicating with your partner, listen with your full presence of being and with genuine curiosity. Being open and receptive to learning about yourself and your partner in the deepest of ways will enhance your intimacy, which is very important for this king.

Wear the Crown

Respect one another. Avoid being bossy and demanding. Be aware of and curb your expectations, as they can be unreasonably high with this king sitting in the throne. Love and compassion stem from respect, and they are the secret keys to the success of this relationship; nothing less will do. It's your responsibility to use love with wisdom when you have this connection with another.

14

Ace of Clubs

The Inquisitive Heart

The Ace of Clubs represents the desire to know, the desire to learn, and the desire to communicate deeply and with great detail. The primary influence carried within this card manifests as a longing to be in union with another; therefore, relationship is very much favored with this connection in the cards. In addition to this driving desire to connect, the Ace of Clubs blesses you and your partner with great emotional compatibility. Often with this connection, there is an undeniable feeling that you are with your soul mate. It's this card's nature to seek emotional compatibility, as its sole purpose is to unite in love; the driving force of this card is to know and to connect.

In this relationship, your partner will satisfy the deep emotional longing that will be ever present in this love connection. Like interests and shared goals, along with nonstop talking and sharing, will be important for the well-being of your relationship. The curious nature of this card's energy creates the need to know what's going on at all times. Depth in interaction and the answers to questions will build and sustain the foundations of your connection together and, at the same time, stabilize your emotions. It's through talking that stability and trust are formed and supported. This card is curious, innocent, and driven by a very intense need for love and companionship, and these characteristics will be present within you and between you.

If you love to talk and enjoy sharing your thoughts, dreams, and ideas, this could be an ideal relationship for you. If that is not the norm for you, this connection could change your behavior in ways that make you more communicative, more curious, and more desirous to unite with another with greater passion than what has been common for you in the past. It's actually a very favorable relationship connection in the cards. So if you're open to being more expressive and communicative, this relationship could be a very auspicious experience—one that enhances your character and your life.

The Ace of Clubs is naturally compelled to gain understanding of the mechanics of relationship. This is actually the innate force driving this card. The inquisitive aspects of this influence will show up in your communication and interaction with one another. Being in this relationship will awaken questions deep within your psyche and bring to the surface things that you might otherwise ignore. It's very likely that your two minds will be stimulated with an ever-present inquisitiveness and curiosity that desire a constant stream of new information and new experiences. For this reason, secrets or hidden agendas will not do, and if such things are brought into the relationship, they will lead each of you into feelings of mistrust and uncertainty that can easily end it.

This connection is ruled by the club suit, which governs the realms of the mind. The sharing of your personal experiences—such as books you've read, lectures you have attended, seminars, and any form of educational event—will be appealing and exciting. Research or attending classes and workshops together will be supportive activities to engage in. Of course, it will be important that these types of events be of personal interest to you. Just know that sharing these types of experiences has the potential to strengthen the bond of love between you like nothing else. This connection could be likened to a freshly plowed field; rows and rows of rich, fertile soil wait to be seeded with new information, learning, and shared experiences, which will lead to an ongoing blessing of great bounty.

Each of you, as an individual, will have a constant need for mental stimulation, the sharing of ideas, and conversation with your partner and with the outside world. The realms of the heart, your feelings, and shared emotions will also be arenas where you spend time exploring. The Ace of Clubs represents the innovative mind of the scientist or investigator, so you can expect a wealth of mental stirring and a great deal of innovative thought. Your minds will be consistently stimulated in new and wonderful directions, even in the realms of business and finance.

The key to making this relationship successful is a solid foundation of friendship. Being friends has to be the first priority. As you foster your friendship, you must remain true to yourself and your individual values. In addition, you will have to establish and keep clear emotional boundaries, as these boundaries will be essential to maintaining your clarity of intention and clear perception relative to your partner.

From time to time, you are likely to find yourselves engaging in arguments, which will be a bit like mental gymnastics. If you choose to argue with wisdom, you will gain from these feisty moments. If you confront one another with kindness—meaning, if you aren't mean—these types of interactions can be a positive aspect for the relationship that keeps things alive and refreshed. You just have to remember to laugh at yourselves in the process in order to keep things light and playful. The secret is not to take yourselves, your feelings, and your ideas about things too seriously.

Nervous energy and restlessness are plentiful with this influence, and if not channeled properly, they can create scattered mental states. Physical activity, both alone and together, will be important to keep the mind in check. Create new adventures, travel, and engage in physical activities like cycling, hiking, horseback riding, swimming, and tennis, for these types of activities will keep your relationship thriving and prevent boredom, which can be a danger with this connection. The Ace of Clubs is extremely fast-moving energy that requires mental challenge and stimulation. Boredom is not acceptable. The challenge in this relationship is to let go of any inhibitions you have surrounding intimacy or trust, and allow yourself take a leap into this wild and wonderful ride. Doing so will become the very thing that unlocks the door to your truest desires.

It could be that you have drawn this relationship to you because you want to learn to allow yourself to feel safe and whole in a partnership that is based on trust—something that perhaps you've not done in the past. You can discover a new realm of intimacy in this relationship if you choose to. Your connection with your partner will provide the perfect playing field for you, and for him or her, to be self-expressive in ways that perhaps weren't possible before. For this reason, it's important to be open to and curious about new forms of expressing yourself. Your partner will have a genuine interest in you, so be receptive and share yourself openly.

Curiosity, receptivity, and trust are your friends in this relationship; give way to them and make them the very foundation of the connection you have with your partner. Choose to let go of old insecurities and self-judgment, and, with this person as your mirror, explore your greatness. These are the opportunities with this connection, and it will be wise of you to take advantage of them.

The Keys to the Kingdom of the Ace of Clubs

Emotional Maturity

Learning to establish and maintain clear emotional boundaries is an important key to making this relationship successful, and it may be something that you need to master. If this is true, you've found a relationship that provides the perfect foundation for making this change in yourself. Grow your emotional maturity with this connection, and this relationship will support you in becoming all that you are.

Best Friends Forever

Friendship is the most important foundation for this connection. Being friends first and lovers second will establish safe, solid ground for each of you to stand on as individuals and together as a couple. Make your partner your very best friend. The fabric of your friendship will bond you together more than anything else possibly can.

Physical Activity

Physical activities must be a vital part of your time spent together. Adventure and exploration fall into this category as well, because the curiosity inherent in this connection must be fed with constant doses of new, uncharted mental, emotional, physical, and spiritual territory. The sometimes-overwhelming influx of mental energy that accompanies this card influence needs physical activity of any and all kinds to dissipate it. Without the physical dispersion of energy the mind will begin to spin out into chaos and distort your emotional perception.

Unquestionable Trust

Trust must live in the belly of this relationship. It's possible that trust has been a past issue for one or both of you, so here you will have a perfect opportunity to learn to let yourself go into intimacy, and to allow yourself to learn to feel emotionally and mentally safe with the unknown.

15

Two of Clubs

Communication—
the Door to the Heart

The Two of Clubs is the card of communication and cooperation. These two elements are the keys to this relationship
happening the way you want it to. You are likely to find yourself talking, talking, and talking because this card is known as the
conversation card. There is another side to this card's influence with
this connection—it can be all too easy to argue. The challenge can
arise through conflicting ideas; the opportunity is to create harmony
and find love through talking about them.

Be patient, reasonable, and attentively aware of any tendencies
toward domination, which can show up quite strongly with this
composite card. The Two of Clubs influence embodies a lot of nervous energy, which has the potential to result in mental and emotional
overreaction. It is helpful to remain aware of this tendency, so that
you can catch it before it gets out of control.

There will be no limit to where you can travel via your communication. And when you explore each other and your relationship in this
way, the creativity and expression that you experience will be unlimited. Connecting openly and with passion creates a natural charge of
electricity that is titillating and spurs each of you into action. Simply
put, you will love, love, love to talk with one another. Take care,
though, as this stimulating energy can also turn into arguments, which

is not its most favorable form of expression. You must maintain mental and emotional balance with your excitement, so that your communication doesn't go from sharing with excitement to a battle of egos and wills, which can happen with the Two of Clubs connection.

The personal need to retreat and be alone, both as a couple and individually, must be honored, as quiet time restores and nurtures each of you and your relationship as a whole. You must be forthcoming and honest with one another and the world, and you cannot keep any secrets from your partner. In the underbelly of this card exists raw fear, which can make you feel mentally uncertain and emotionally unstable without notice. This underlying fear explains the need for constant communication, openness, and honesty, as these are the things that keep the fear at bay.

Cooperation is the key to success in this partnership. It's a great connection to have in a relationship as long as you value the depth at which you can really connect and share.

The Keys to the Kingdom of the Two of Clubs

Commitment to Cooperation

As a result of being under the influence of this card, you both might find that you're more sensitive than usual when you are together. Take care, and remember that the opportunity is to become more aware of each other and others in general. Your awareness is being fine-tuned. Commit to participating in this change, otherwise arguments will brew, and your minds will wobble.

Time Alone

Solitude is a must. Time alone and time practicing meditation, doing yoga, or being in nature are important for both of you as individuals. Give one another space and support for these methods of rejuvenation so that you can each be more present and giving in your relationship.

Home as Your Sanctuary

Home is your castle. It must be a sanctuary where you find restoration and nurturing. Surround yourselves with beauty and harmony in all ways—visually and through sound, touch, and fragrance. Fresh, moving air and plenty of light are needed to create a harmonious, nurturing environment, which will ease the innate nervous energy of the Two of Clubs's influence.

Sharing What's Important

Shared values are necessary to create a strong foundation with this connection. You must have things of importance in common. If these things are lacking, find them or create them. Life has to be more than just mundane with this connection. Use your shared mental genius to create abundance for others.

16
Three of Clubs
The Sensitive Mind

This is the card of mental creativity, and it's commonly referred to as the writer's card. Its influence is filled with imagination, creativity, and self-expression, all of which will be vital aspects of your relationship. On the higher side of its expression, this energy is highly imaginative, playful, and creative; it's also magnetic. In this relationship it will be imperative that you take care to be sensitive with one another in your communication, and engage in physical and mental activities to insure emotional balance and mental stability.

The challenging side of this relationship could manifest as an underlying feeling of uncertainty that each of you has regarding the relationship. If you allow tension to build in your environment, or if you focus on the uncertainty or insecurity that can arise with this composite card, the relationship will begin to deteriorate. Exploding anger, conflict, misunderstanding, indecision, and worry are the negatives that can influence this relationship and make it a challenge.

The secret to success lies in keeping a positive, forward-moving attitude in expressing your affection and kindness to one another. You must keep the channels of communication open so that each of you knows what the other is thinking and feeling. This type of communication helps to stabilize the not-so-stable mind of the Three of Clubs. The Three of Clubs energy has its own brand of acute sensitivity, and that energy will rise to the surface of your conscious minds and express itself. Avoid focusing on what worries you or how your needs aren't being met, as this kind of thinking will spiral you straight into mental anxiety. Instead, think about new and exciting ways to spend time together, and focus on how much you love your partner. It can take work to keep this relationship afloat, but it will be worth it. It's all about keeping the energy up and being kind to one another.

Joint creative endeavors are highly favored with this connection. There can be opportunities for financial growth and success or for a prosperous business partnership. Communication is the magic wand. The secret to making this relationship successful is to seek a deeper understanding of the emotional needs that you and your partner each have. This exploration will be your best investment.

You will have the opportunity to explore and discover how to raise the bar on your values, and to explore new ways of thinking as an individual and as a couple. This relationship cannot be done in a traditional way. It's about creativity, exploration, constant change, movement, communication, and expression of the self. If you honor all of these things and incorporate them into your relationship, and if you can live with recurring feelings of uncertainty, you will have a very dynamic and wonderful relationship. If you have expectations and want this person to fit into a conceptual box of how you think things should be, this relationship will never bring you the satisfaction you desire.

The opportunity you have in this relationship is to become freer in your self-expression. Step outside your concepts of how you think a relationship is supposed to be, and explore new aspects of yourself that take you beyond insecurities you have regarding intimacy and trust. Approaching the relationship from this angle will bring you new awareness and new ways of being with yourself, along with enhanced sensitivity in all your relationships with others.

The fact that you are drawn to this relationship says that you want to seek deeper meaning in your life and know what is true and real for you. Your spirit is calling to you to seek and find what your truest expression is and how you might manifest it. Writing, such as journaling, can help to bring you clarity and a deeper connection with your innermost desires.

The Keys to the Kingdom of the Three of Clubs

Commitment to Kindness

Kindness and sensitivity are of the utmost importance in this relationship. You must do your best to be open and loving even when you feel afraid. Be affectionate and compassionate.

Understanding Appreciation

Show your partner that you are grateful for him or her on a regular basis. Give, even when you think you should be receiving, as you cannot be too giving with this connection. Understand that expressions of appreciation and gratitude are the golden tickets to your partner's heart. The Three of Clubs is a fragile energy that needs a constant outward expression of love.

Taking Initiative

It's necessary to create new and different experiences together and to make things happen, rather than just expecting them to. So you must remember to take the initiative to create new opportunities for sharing. The best measure is for both of you to assume 100 percent of the responsibility for creating your happiness together.

Selective Self-Expression

Say what you feel, say what you think, and express who you are, while giving your partner room to do the same. Just be sure that you do these things in a way that creates harmony rather than confusion or doubt. Independence and freedom of expression are gems that must be valued, and they must be guided by awareness and kindness.

17
Four of Clubs
Mental Structures

The Four of Clubs symbolizes the stable mind, and it carries with it a natural ability to organize thoughts and bring ideas into form. Clubs represent the mental realm, and culture, language, communication, and intelligence will be key interests for this relationship. These elements could very well be the basis of your connection with each other, as well as part of the environment in which you first met.

Socializing with friends and making new acquaintances will be common occurrences during your relationship. Home life will be a significant focus of your time as well, and comfort in your home will be an absolutely necessity. Your surroundings will be balanced, lovely, and harmonious.

Clear and precise communication with one another must be at the foundation of this connection; without it your relationship will deteriorate. Take the time to clearly see who your partner is and hear what he or she has to say, as there is a tendency with the Four of Clubs influence to have veiled vision when it comes to love. If you're not honest with yourself regarding how you see your partner, it could be all too easy to see what you want to see and ignore those things that you intuitively know could lead to challenges and ultimately misfortune. Be real with yourself and him or her, and if something doesn't feel right, talk about it immediately. Deception is unforgivable and will certainly undermine the integrity of this partnership, leading straight to its demise. Honesty begins with your own perception.

Another challenge that can present itself when this card governs a relationship is strange or unusual circumstances occurring unexpectedly. These occurrences could happen on a fairly frequent basis. Change can take place when you least expect it as well, so pay attention and do your best to respond with your intelligence rather than your emotions. When these situations arise, be open and receptive to the changes and surprises that life brings your way, and do your best to see the gifts that they offer, even though those gifts may sometimes be disguised.

If you're presently in this relationship and finding things a bit challenging, take some time to think about what your personal long-term goals are. Do they match your partner's? Do the two of you share the same values in life? It's vital for the life of your relationship that you share common goals and like values. Also ask yourself if things are actually as they seem. Be certain that you're not seeing the relationship through rose-colored glasses—seeing what you want to see rather than what's actually happening. The Four of Clubs can be deaf, dumb, and blind when it comes to having clarity in love. The element of deception or delusion is very strong; to find clarity and use wisdom, we must act as masterful detectives with our own perception.

Always, always, always trust your intuition! If you feel something is off or amiss, it most likely is, and you must check it out. If it feels on, know that it is right. Trusting your gut feelings is the bottom line with this connection. Once you're clear in your own mind, openly and honestly communicate what is important to you. If you find yourself justifying, rationalizing, or telling yourself stories to support what you want or think is going on, you are not being honest with yourself. If you don't have to justify your thinking to feel comfortable, then you are free to rise to the higher side of this card influence, which is extremely intuitive, creative, and productive.

Spend quiet time together to revitalize your relationship. If you find that things feel strained, spend some time together at home sharing in a way that you both enjoy. Or go out into nature—take a walk, a bike ride, or do whatever you like doing together. Time together is important for this relationship to be healthy and thriving. Also remember that your home environment is extremely important. You will thrive when you are surrounded by beauty and harmony.

You may have called this relationship to yourself to refine your mind and to establish new ways of communicating who you are and what you want in your life. These are things that can certainly be accomplished in this relationship. Mental and physical discipline is called for with the Four of Clubs connection, and both are important for mental-emotional balance and good physical health.

By all means, avoid aggressive communication or arguing for the sake of being right. The choice is between being right and being loved. And it is a choice—one that must be made moment by moment. If you observe yourself getting stuck in this mental battle, give in and choose love.

Doing something out of the ordinary is a great way to revive the relationship if it's stuck in a rut. Remain aware of and do your best to avoid power struggles, ego battles, anger, and addictions, if these are habits that you possess. Those things will pull the bottom out from under this relationship. When you choose positive attitudes, anything is possible. Do the opposite, and all will be lost and you have to begin again. This dance of positive versus negative can happen over and over if you don't resonate with the higher vibrations of the card.

On the other hand, this partnership can be a very solid foundation for having a family, raising children, and creating a stable home life. If you've been looking for a partnership in which you work with your mate, this could be a good one for that as well, and a lucrative one indeed. Focus and determination in material directions can bring great good fortune and long-lasting success.

The Keys to the Kingdom of the Four of Clubs

Intuitive Intelligence

Intuition plays a major role in this relationship. Each of you must draw on your intuitive intelligence and follow its guidance implicitly, so that you can make choices and decisions based on what you feel and know is right in the belly of your being. The mind can play tricks on the Four of Clubs when it's not anchored in the intelligence of the body, so cultivate this awareness in a balanced way. Don't throw your logic out the window; rather, let your logical mind be the copilot, covering your intuitive decisions in realistic ways.

Choosing Love

Be honest, open, and clear. Under this card's influence, it's very easy to become a bit fixed or stubborn with your own opinions. Be receptive and listen when communicating with your partner, otherwise egos will run amuck. If you have past emotional issues that you need to clear up, don't do it in the relationship. Instead, do it on your own or with a therapist, so that the information you share with your partner has to do with him or her and not something or someone from the past. Remember: choose being loved over being right!

Nurture Yourselves with Nature

Nurturing one another is a key element in insuring security with this connection. Spending time in nature will be equally nourishing for each of you and the two of you as a couple. The energy that you find there will help ground and stabilize your relationship. Indoor and outdoor activities and events—anything that feeds your intelligence and sense of beauty—are favored. Avoid letting your life together become stagnant or routine. Action and change are essential for this connection to thrive.

Home

Your home has great significance and is meant to be a sanctuary for your love. Surround yourself with your favorite colors, fabrics, shapes, sounds, and smells. Home is where you rejuvenate yourselves and your connection. Create the perfect space to house your partnership. Beauty and harmony must be at the very foundation of this relationship.

18
Five of Clubs
The Curiosity of Love

The Five of Clubs is known as the card of mental adventure. Having this card as a relationship ruler means that you're in for a wild ride that could bring about changes in the way you think and possibly in how you perceive yourself and the world around you. You might find that you become more physically and mentally active, more curious and exploratory, and more open and interested in experiencing change in a variety of ways. In this relationship you can expect life overall, and plans in general, to change often.

You might have felt that you already knew this person when first you met. That's because there is an element of destiny embodied in this connection. This meeting was meant to be. What you do with it is a choice you each make for yourselves.

There is a very dreamy quality that lives in this connection, and along with that comes a danger of becoming lost in fantasy and sometimes-unrealistic ways of thinking. It's possible that this will occur on a somewhat regular basis, so you will have to keep your imagination in check. Even though it's okay to enjoy seeing the world through your new rose-colored glasses, you also will want to stay grounded in reality, so that you make clear choices for yourself and together.

Fives represent change and experience, and they are symbols of the human journey through life. Humanity is here to develop, learn, and evolve through life experiences. When you enter a five relationship, you can bet that there will be a lot going on and that you will be learning through all of your experiences. Change is the master operator of the five influence, and you will find that the secret to success in this relationship lies in being flexible, malleable, and acquiescent.

The ability to be financially creative is one of the gifts of this card, and when put to the task, this influence can easily lead to good fortune and increased finances. If this energy is not focused and channeled, money worries may be an undermining factor between the two of you. So if you find yourself worrying about financial issues, it's a sign that you are not making use of the creative financial intelligence living within this card's influence. It would be wise—and possibly lucrative—to draw upon the creative intelligence this card has to offer.

There is a strong element of personal transformation that comes by way of new learning experiences, along with a constant review and renewal of spiritual and material values. The Five of Clubs is innately inspired, and its inspiration may evoke the desire to accomplish something important. Attaining and maintaining your focus on the goals that you set for yourself might be a challenge, as distraction is a strong characteristic of this card. Focused intention will help you get on track, and once you're locked in, it's more than possible to attain anything you set your mind to.

The playful spirit and creative intelligence of this card will have the two of you being anything but bored. Conversation will be exciting and constant, and, as long as you choose to give way to one another, you'll be able to avoid arguments. If you get too serious in this relationship, you'll spoil the connection. The Five of Clubs likes to play, so give the childlike innocence of your spirit permission to be free, as it is safe to do so here.

It's through reinvention of self and re-creation of life that this relationship finds its way through time to longevity. Creativity is the key that will unlock the secret expression of this partnership. The reward, if you choose to rise to the occasions that change presents to the two of you, is a loving connection that is innocent and fun. Just be sure that you are realistic in your choices and open and honest with each other.

If you are currently in this relationship, and you are experiencing challenges or questioning it in some way, try applying the advice that you find here to support what the relationship really needs. Do this from your heart. The Five of Clubs is very innocent energy, and there must be openness and curiosity present between you. If you don't feel secure in this relationship, either it's not the best place for you or perhaps you need to let your innocence come forth. Only you know which is true for you.

If you are considering this relationship, think carefully. If you like change and are comfortable with the unexpected, this connection can be an exciting adventure. If you like adventure and are comfortable with the unknown, this is a place where you can explore yourself, life, and relationship in new and exciting ways. However, if change is not your cup of tea, perhaps a more solid type of relationship would be better for you. The Five of Clubs relationship can be unsettling though for those who like to have their feet firmly planted on the ground. On the other hand, it could be that you need a little loosening up, and that's why you attracted this person your way.

The Keys to the Kingdom of the Five of Clubs

Focused Intention

In this relationship you will have the opportunity to learn to use your determination to create and maintain your mental focus and the application of your intention. The nature of this card has a tendency to scatter mental energy, which in turn creates distractions on a consistent basis. The exercise will be to walk a fine line of mental discipline and to support your partner in doing the same, in whatever ways are most beneficial and necessary. Those ways must also be enjoyable, of course, as this card prefers enjoyment.

Expanding Creativity

Creative ideas will come easily, and the best thing you can do when they show up is capture them and give them a home. This is especially true if they have to do with making money, because this card likes to play with money and is very good at attracting it and keeping track of it. Creativity of any kind will do, though, and any type of creative expression will make you both happy.

Adventure

You must plan adventures, travel, and find new and unusual things to do to stimulate your minds and keep your passion alive. Often with this connection, the more unusual the things you engage in, the greater the rewards. Keep moving. This card is known as the Adventurer, and it's important to stir the pot if things become routine.

Giving Way

This is a golden key to making this relationship grand. Give way to the innocence of your spirit when you are with your partner, and in return you will experience greatest happiness. Look deeply to see who is behind those eyes—the ones you fell in love with—and give way to your heart.

19

Six *of* Clubs

Dreaming Reality

Destiny is at work with this connection, and it's clear that you were meant to come together in some way. The question is, in which way? Clarity is a key determinant with this connection. Clear, shoot-from-the-hip, present-in-the moment communication is absolutely necessary in this relationship.

This is a dreamy, artistic card, which can be prone to escapism, irresponsibility, and laziness, so you must take care to keep things moving in the direction of reality. Practice and diligence will be needed to see things as they really are, rather than getting lost in fantasy and illusion. You will love being in love, and you will thrive on the romance and beauty of it all. Ultimately, this can be a magnificent connection; it's just a matter of keeping things in a realistic perspective.

The creative intelligence found with this connection can bring about some excellent financial opportunities and rewards. The Six of Clubs is a very fortunate card. Action will be the key to bringing that fortune to fruition. Balancing your love life with work and the practical applications of your imagination, and then choosing to take action with your ideas, will be what brings forth fulfillment. There is an abundance of inspiration and imagination at work here, and when put into form, it can yield wonderful benefits.

The dreamy energy of the six has a tendency to gravitate toward stillness rather than action, so you'll have to practice being consistent

LOVE AND DESTINY

107

with your effort to put things into motion. You will have to be diligent about keeping your relationship hot and juicy, as this is what sparks the creative expressions that lead to good fortune. You must take action to reap the rewards, and that action must be practical. *Action* is, undeniably and always, the key!

If you are presently in this relationship, be sure to keep things moving, and take action to continuously bring new energy into the partnership. The mind of the Six of Clubs is extremely agile and highly imaginative. Balance the constant need for stimulation and input with quiet, reflective moments, and always put your ideas into action. Follow-through will be the challenge, as well as the opportunity.

Dream together and then do something about your dreams. Then repeat. It's all too easy with this influence to just dream and leave it at that. Dreams without action will eventually lead to boredom, which will deteriorate the very core of your connection.

If you are considering this relationship, be sure to pull your head out of the clouds long enough to realistically look at it and determine if it's right for you. It was surely the hand of fate that brought you together; just be clear about your choices as you move forward. This can be a great relationship, as long as you base it in reality not fantasy.

The Keys to the Kingdom of the Six of Clubs

Take Action Now

Take it! This can be a very lethargic influence, which can cause you to become lazy and, for some, inactive. Procrastination is a favorite choice for this card, so taking action with your ideas when you have them is extremely important. If you find that you are becoming complacent, do something about it, because if you don't, eventually things will decline into total boredom.

Drama-Free Zone

Be open and honest with one another without sharing everything that's on your mind. Avoid drama and crazy behavior at all costs. This card has an extremely low tolerance for both.

Reality versus Fantasy

Be realistic and practical in your choices together. This card can create dreamy illusions. Remember to remove the rose-colored glasses from time to time to conduct reality checks.

Sharing Your Wisdom

The Six of Clubs is actually known as the Messenger. It's likely that you and your partner will have many inspired moments together under this card influence. The higher side of this card says, "When inspired, share what you learn and know with your partner and others."

20
Seven *of* Clubs

Refinement of the Mind

The Seven of Clubs is the representative of spiritual knowledge and the refined mind. Given this card's influences, you will need to walk a fine line in order to maintain its higher qualities within a partnership. There will be emphasis on all things having to do with the mind, which include learning, education, communication, and inspiration. Honesty will be tested repeatedly in this relationship. Something else that will be highlighted is any negative beliefs that either one of you adheres to. These will be revealed and challenged. Obsessive behaviors, overindulgence, and overspending can emerge with this connection and will be the very things that undermine the core of the relationship.

All of this sounds a bit heavy, I know. Fortunately, there's another side to this relationship. When you live free from the ego, interact with spontaneity, accept one another, and let go of the need to be in control, you will experience a partnership that is alive and electric. Additionally, when you learn to create as partners, your relationship will be the perfect platform for manifesting all of your dreams. The secret to attaining this level of satisfaction and good fortune will be found in letting go of the need to be in control, while also choosing to be forthright with yourself and you partner.

Seven-based relationships can be a bit challenging. This one will demand that you refine how you use your thinking and how you live relative to your beliefs. On the high side of things, the seven is very spiritual. When aligned with its energy, you will grow personally and spiritually by leaps and bounds, making significant headway with your personal self-mastery. When you're not aligned with the higher energy of this card, obstacles will and often do occur. These obstacles are present to turn you around and direct you inward, so that you distill your mind and rid it of any negative or unproductive beliefs, attitudes, and behaviors. When you do the work, you will reap the rewards. The rewards are rich experiences of your creative expression, financial success, and deep personal satisfaction. If you fail do the work suggested by this card, just the opposite will manifest.

If you're presently in this relationship, seriously consider what is being said here. It always pays to take the high road with the cards, and the opportunities for self-awareness and self-mastery are endless with this connection. If a path of self-awareness isn't your focus at the moment, then it is possible that you can attain mastery with business and finance. The energy of the Seven of Clubs can be extremely manipulative. It's unacceptable to use this energy to manipulate others as this behavior undermines our lives and comes back to haunt us. However, when this energy is focused toward personal or professional growth, great blessings and recognition are bestowed.

If you are considering this relationship, know that it is a powerful connection, and when used in the highest ways, both in the personal and professional realms, you can make great gains. Your opportunity will be to let go of some old ways of doing things while simultaneously adopting new behaviors and new ways of thinking. There is a good deal of passion that will come forth in this relationship, and, when channeled, it can serve you in many ways.

The Keys to the Kingdom of the Seven of Clubs

Passion

Channel your mutual passion in ways that support the creation of whatever it is that your hearts desire. Passion and sensuality are strong elements in this connection, so use them wisely and creatively rather than becoming consumed by them to the point of overindulgence. Enjoy and create!

Surrender

For this relationship to be successful, you must surrender your ego and the need to be in control. Working in partnership will put you on your greatest path to success. If you fail to join in your efforts, respect one another, and acknowledge each other's personal strengths, power struggles will chip away at the very foundation of your love.

Creative Expansion

The two of you can move mountains when you are in sync with one another and aligned with your higher goals—the power of one plus one turns into the power of eleven. This is a major secret that awaits your discovery in this relationship. When your joint creativity is put into motion, you will become unstoppable, and there will be no limits to what you can accomplish together. Fame and recognition can be a result of these types of efforts.

Right Use of Power

Inner reflection and mental refinement will be ongoing processes for each of you. It's imperative that you refine your beliefs and your thought patterns, as doing so will set you free of old habits and old ways of thinking that no longer serve you or your future. This card represents spiritual knowledge and the refinement of the mind. You must have clarity of purpose and a mutual sharing of values for the greatest success in this relationship. If the aforementioned path is not the choice, the power of this card can easily be misused.

21

Eight of Clubs

The Power of Intention

The Eight of Clubs is the card of mental intention and material accomplishment through the application of the focused mind. This card embodies strong, determined mental energy. The power of this card operates solely through its fixed nature. Being governed by this influence in a relationship can bring about some head-to-head combat in the realm of communication, and as a result there will be many opportunities for self-reflection and learning that come through your personal interaction.

This can be a very juicy connection—one that is filled with unending passion and intent. The highest law of the land of this relationship is honesty. Hidden issues, such as anger from the past, will quickly be revealed and have to be dealt with. The most productive ways to move through these challenging times is to face them with an open mind and honest communication. Each of you will show the strongest aspects of your personal will in this relationship, and each of you will have the opportunity to learn how to be in partnership with more compassion and grace. You will accomplish this learning by choosing to be more flexible and receptive, which is not an easy task with this card at the helm. I don't want to make this connection sound like one of doom and gloom, because it's not. It's more like swoon and boom! And you never know when which one is coming.

This connection can be a magical ride if you meet eye to eye, mind to mind, and heart to heart. Being open to one another's ideas and adaptable in your thinking is the key to the success of your relationship. There is much protection and good fortune that surrounds this connection; the secret to allowing good fortune to come your way is simply a matter of taking off the hard hats and opening up the heart. The Eight of Clubs has a slightly obsessive disposition, and the characteristics of this temperament can create challenges in the relationship. You must take care to avoid adopting obsessive behaviors, attitudes, or even addictions, as these things will deteriorate your connection immediately and create unimaginable chaos. For most, obsession and addiction are not a problem. However, if you or your partner have an addictive personality or challenges with obsession, the energies lying under the surface of this card can bring those individual tendencies up and out. The opportunity here is to recognize and deal with them.

If you are in this relationship, the secret to making it successful is in the ownership of your personal power and your ability to maintain clear boundaries, while simultaneously expressing your love, affection, acceptance, and support for your partner.

If you're finding yourself overreacting toward your partner, you may have some unresolved anger issues. And if you do, this relationship connection will surely bring them front and center to be addressed. If this is happening, take personal responsibility for dealing with your anger. Once you've identified its source and cleared it, then you can resume clear communication with your partner. This is not the easiest of relationship paths, because the personal will becomes stronger than usual under this influence. However, if you and your partner focus your intention together in the same direction, this path can be amazingly successful and totally blessed, and it will bring you great good fortune.

If you're considering this relationship, know that it's not the easiest one in the deck. It will push you in ways you may not have been pushed before. This could be the very reason you're drawn to it, so pay attention and avoid making unreasonable compromises. Abuse of any kind is unacceptable. Ultimately, this can be a very empowering relationship if honesty, self-respect, and clear communication are valued and respected as most important. At the same time, you must know that it will always take work to maintain a gracious, loving connection in this relationship.

The Keys to the Kingdom of the Eight of Clubs

Letting Your Guard Down

The Eight of Clubs has within its character a strong predisposition for battle. It is one of the most willful cards in the deck. The act of letting down your guard and being open and receptive will have to be practiced repeatedly. The personal will is the master player in this relationship, and you, its keeper, must be aware when it tries to take over. Stepping back and becoming the observer will be imperative, without exception.

Focused Intention

Mental focus is the power inherent in this card, and the Eight of Clubs relationship will certainly bless you with its strength. The danger is when that focus becomes too myopic or willful. In order to access this energy in constructive and productive ways, you must have goals and intentions that you set for yourself, for your communication with your partner, and for your relationship. Setting these goals must be done as individuals and as a couple.

Honesty

Honesty is like a magic carpet and a safety net at the same time. Even the smallest deviation from the absolute truth will begin unraveling the core foundation of your connection. Be honest with yourself and be honest with your partner, no matter what. Intuition is a strong characteristic of the Eight of Clubs, so any hidden agendas will be felt and will create mistrust, which will be very difficult, if not impossible, to turn around.

Self-Respect

This is, first and foremost, the key to making this relationship all it can be. Your self-respect, or lack thereof, will be reflected back to you in the ways your partner treats you. Each of you must respect yourself, your personal boundaries, and your emotional needs in this partnership. This connection is not for the weak. And if you have issues with self-esteem, they will surely make themselves available for you to do something about them. I would suggest taking advantage of the powerful influence of the Eight of Clubs to make positive changes in your reality. This card has the power to move mountains, so what's a little self-doubt? Employ this card's energy with gratitude.

22
Nine of Clubs
Choosing to Participate

This is a very karmic type of relationship, and it's likely that your meeting couldn't have been avoided, even if you'd tried. Passion and desire are strong with this connection; it's dreamy, romantic, and totally unpredictable.

When engaged in a Nine of Clubs relationship, you will have to let go of how you think things are meant to be and how you want them to be. There are a lot of demands that come standard with this connection. You will have to be receptive to life's agenda, rather than yours. You will have to stay balanced and grounded within yourself, because the sexual desire that manifests in a Nine of Clubs relationship can lead to serious overindulgence, which can lead to ill health or poor choices regarding other things. At the same time, you will have to be open to exploring and discovering new ways of expressing yourselves, as inhibitions will stall the higher energy of this connection and lead to its decline. Balance is the key for the mental and emotional health of this relationship, because it's not the easiest one to be in.

Power struggles are common with this connection, and you will need to take care that communication doesn't become distasteful or mean. Old patterns and past fears regarding love and intimacy are up for review here; they must be looked at seriously and then brought to conscious awareness so they can be shifted. As with all nines, endings and beginnings are constants, and they will be realities for the duration of this relationship. However, endings pave avenues for new beginnings, and with this connection the new beginnings will have to do with your self-respect and how you relate to love and intimacy. These experiences will tap on the door of your heart and its deepest desires. You will ask, "What do I truly want for myself?"

The Nine of Clubs character can fall prey to becoming a victim. Living in the victim consciousness is unattractive and completely disempowering, and doing so is a choice that we make. Embrace the lessons that come with this card and the opportunities for unfolding your truest essence, and you will be blessed. This relationship can grow stronger with time; you just have to play by the rules of the Nine of Clubs, which is to let go and open your mind to greater possibilities—constantly and repeatedly. Along with those lessons comes the choice to be either a participant in your life or a victim of circumstance. If you find yourself choosing to be a victim, stop it immediately and look at the choices you are making. You have the power to make your life whatever you want it to be. It is not up to someone else. It could be that you've drawn this relationship in your direction to become more consciously aware of your true ability to create your life as you want it.

If you are presently in this relationship, understanding the influences this card brings with it will be extremely helpful. It's not an easy relationship to be in, because you are not allowed to bring the past with you—at all. Anything hanging around from the past will be spotted and brought up for reevaluation. You have to deal with your old issues, and if you don't, things can become *extremely* unpleasant. As long as you make the decision to participate in the creation of your life, let go of old issues and expectations, and open yourself up to the new and the unknown, you will be rewarded with a deeper experience of self-awareness and self-respect, and you will create a stronger foundation for love in the relationship.

If you are not conscious in this relationship, you will experience great disappointment and struggle. On the high side of things, the

Nine of Clubs is a very spiritual card; it represents consciousness and understanding. However, in order to tap into its energies, you have to make conscious effort. What is the effort? Being kind to yourself and to your partner, and letting go of any and all associations with being a victim rather than taking responsibility for creating your life.

If you are considering entering into this relationship, bear in mind what is being said here and think long and hard. This isn't an easy relationship to be in. You may want to take the time to be sure that the passion and desire you are feeling have some substance behind them before you jump in all the way. It can be a great sexual relationship; however, once the knot is tied, it can become a living hell if you are not choosing conscious awareness. The only reason this might not happen is if the two of you have otherwise very favorable connections in your life paths, or if you are jointly traveling a path of spirituality. Then the Nine of Clubs relationship can be amazing.

The Keys to the Kingdom of the Nine of Clubs

Being in the Present

Healing past emotional wounds and giving yourself permission to learn a new way of being in a relationship are major lessons that you can learn with this connection, and these very experiences will teach you to live more fully in the present. The Nine of Clubs tells us to let go of our old ways of thinking, our old beliefs, and our expectations of how things are supposed to be. Your opportunity in this relationship is learning to be more present in your life.

Spiritual Values

The Nine of Clubs is a powerfully spiritual card and one that initiates us, if we so choose to engage it, into more expansive ways of thinking. The choice is always between being a victim and being a participant. The higher side of this card represents a shift into higher consciousness, and if the two of you are on some sort of spiritual path together, this path will take the relationship out of the realm of challenge and into great expanse and love. This shifting into new awareness will be seen in your communication as well.

Balance of Mind, Body, and Spirit

You must strive to have balance in body, mind, and spirit in order to avoid overindulgence. Without this balance, things will tilt so far off course that it will be hard to bring them back. Seek to experience and express your greatest integrity in this relationship. You have to be strong in this way because life will go to ruin if there is not self-discipline with regard to indulgence and deception.

Kindness

You must choose to be kind and express that kindness in all ways possible. The most effective way to conjure kindness is through gratitude. Focus on what you appreciate about your partner and your relationship, as doing so will increase your capacity to express your love. In order to be kind to someone else, you must first be kind to yourself. The way to create kindness in your relationship is to establish and maintain clear emotional boundaries for yourself. From that place of self-respect, you will then choose kindness in your communication. In this relationship connection, kindness is the healer and the promoter of love and respect.

23

Ten *of* Clubs

Teaching through Generosity

The Ten of Clubs is a card of forthrightness, diligence, and honor. Deep within the spirit of this card lives a driving desire to make the world a better place, one person at a time. The intelligence of this card is blessed with a global perspective that knows how life can be better and what is needed to bring that improvement about. This card represents the gathering of minds, and it seeks to find those who think like it does. In this relationship, you will find yourselves expanding your circles of thought and your circles of interaction with the world at large.

Embedded within this connection is the opportunity to gain self-mastery. Because this card is of the club suit, that mastery is gained in the realm of the mind and all things within the mind's domain. The Ten of Clubs embodies a hard-working, diligent ethic—one that is progressive and spurred into action by generosity. So the more attention you place on your personal development, the more comfortable you will be in this relationship. Shared spiritual values will be an absolute must. Giving to others will become a habit.

Taking time to communicate is the very most important commitment you can make to your partner, and communication must be the foundation on which your connection is built. The individualist nature of this card will cause you to be more independent. It's all too easy for the Ten of Clubs to put a schedule in motion and expect everyone else to go along with the program. Be careful that you don't fall prey to this workaholic-type tendency.

Change, especially through travel, will bring pleasure and lightness into your connection with one another. There is an abundance of creative energy available, and you may have to make effort to take the time to explore that energy, since you can get carried away with work. Forming a business partnership together can be a major success, as long as you use your enthusiasm to recognize the power your partner has to bring forth his or her ideas. And, of course, this support will have to go both ways.

Personal freedom and independence will be important for each of you. If you want to be in a relationship where the relationship itself is the focus, you are in the wrong place here. Freedom of being is the most important thing for individuals and relationships governed by this card. Maintaining your individuality and independence while being together with your partner will work great. Conventional or traditional forms of relating may not fare as well in this relationship and, if expected, could cause frustration and disappointment. Emotional dependency does not work in this environment. Consequently, this relationship can be a bit of a balancing act at times. You will appreciate the traditional ways of being together, and at the same time, each of you will have the need to express who you are as an individual. Personal experience means everything for each of you with this connection, and you will be happiest when you have your personal priorities at the top of the list. Dress your experiences in something new on a regular basis—meaning create new and different things to do together.

If you are presently in this relationship, realize that the Ten of Clubs does not like to be tied down, and that your relationship will thrive on mutual respect for each other's personal freedom. I don't mean open dating, although some may choose to do that. What I'm really speaking about is freedom from codependency. This partnership will not conform to anyone's expectations or fit into some familiar box. Freedom and independence will give this relationship room to breathe, allowing each of you space to grow and become more of who you really are. The stronger your individuality, the greater your magnetism with your partner.

If you are exploring the possibilities of this relationship, know that if you want a traditional type of relationship, you might be barking up the wrong tree. If you love your independence and you can support your partner having his or her independence, then you can go far and have wonderful experiences that expand your mind and your self-expression. If you are already in this relationship and experiencing challenges, please take to heart the message here. If you find it enlightening, apply the Keys to the Kingdom and see what happens. You have the power to take your relationship wherever you want it to go—you just have to play by the rules of the game as written by the Ten of Clubs.

The Keys to the Kingdom of the Ten of Clubs

Openness and Receptivity

Let go of any need to be in control, and enjoy the new realms of creative thinking and dynamic communication that this relationship has to offer. Communication is the master key of this relationship, and the highest form of communication will happen when you are open, receptive, and present.

Individual Independence

Honor your own freedom to be, as well as that of your partner. This card's energy can encourage greater independence, along with enhanced strength of will and character. It's a powerful individual influence in this way, and as a relationship influence, it can bring about some wonderful new ways of relating.

Self-Discovery

This is a major key. Explore new ways of being together, new ways of communicating, new learning about intimacy and sexuality; whatever your explorations may be, use the energy of this Ten of Clubs to discover new things about yourself, replace old things that no longer serve you, and start life anew every day.

Financial Creativity

Working in partnership—whether that partnership is a global effort, project, or business—can give this relationship a real charge and keep things moving in a positive and lucrative direction. The only challenge here can be power struggles. Simply avoid them by employing your intelligence in greater ways.

24
Jack of Clubs
The Eclectic Journey

This connection can be like a wild magnetic storm of attraction and desire. Sparks can fly, and electricity will fill the air. However, all of this may be observed by each of you personally from a slightly removed perspective, as this jack can be a bit aloof. This is a unique type of energy for a relationship, and one that is beyond interesting to explore.

The Jack of Clubs is the card of mental genius and creativity, and this jack hosts a fast-moving mental energy that is stimulating and eclectic. When it comes to love, the Jack of Clubs has a tendency to do it differently from the rest of the deck, so you will have to stay alert at all times if you have this connection in the cards. I say this because this jack tends to draw on logic and intelligence rather than emotion when interacting. When applied to an intimate relationship, this tendency can create a very different dynamic from what most experience in a relationship. The unique energetic quality that exists in this relationship connection can be a great platform on which to position yourself as an individual. Emotional drama will not have a place in this relationship. So if you are prone to being emotionally dramatic and you thrive on those types of experiences, forget it.

Freedom and individuality will be major issues for both of you. Anything that gets in the way of personal freedom will automatically be dubbed as an obstacle. You will be asked to exercise your spontaneity in this relationship—period. It's all about the moment. And things will constantly change—often unexpectedly. So if you're comfortable with uncertainty, this relationship could be exciting. If not, it might feel like a nightmare of unpredictability.

The energy of this card can be exhilarating, stimulating, and electrifying. The innate drive within this influence is masterful at creating change. The planet Uranus rules this card, and this planet is famous for destroying old patterns. I can guarantee that old patterns or issues having to do with relationships, or even who you think you might be, will not survive here. Tradition does not work with this connection either. Letting go of how you think things are supposed to be and how you've done them in the past is the means by which you make this relationship fly—and it will do just that. If you don't let go of the past or your old ways of thinking and relating, your expectations will bring disappointment and grief, seemingly out of nowhere. If you do let go of these things, you will have great conversations that explore every aspect of life and encourage new avenues for exploration and self-expression.

You might find that you feel a bit detached in this relationship. That is the Jack of Clubs mental approach to love. It's best to simply observe this new behavior, if you experience it, and know that it's quite normal with this connection. You will be led to experiment and engage with every aspect of your life in a brand new way. New social adventures, going places you have not been before, or doing things you would not normally do—all of these will be very important to keeping this relationship alive and well. Be original. Be spontaneous. And do things that inspire you and your partner. All of the aforementioned will be true for the inner worlds of your mind and emotions as well.

Expansive thought and deep communication are the blood of this connection, and emotional issues must be handled through the logic department rather the drama department. The Jack of Clubs does not compute feelings in the same way the rest of the pack does. It is through creative intelligence and critical thinking that all issues are reviewed and all problems are solved. Therefore, it's crucial that you cultivate your understanding of this dynamic. And always expect the unexpected, as *change* will govern the very foundation of your connection with one another.

If you are presently in this relationship, you have a wonderful opportunity to access and express your unique individuality unlike ever before. This connection will stir your individuality loose in your deepest, innermost psyche. Take chances and step outside the box. Live on the edge of the unknown, claim your own distinctive expression of self, and create your personal signature, while also supporting the uniqueness of your partner's character. Talk, share, be, and play in new realms on a consistent basis—this will keep things alive and juicy. This card is directly plugged into raw intelligence and the outer realms of the higher mind. Its expression of this intelligence is eclectic, unpredictable, and ever changing, and so will your relationship be.

If you are considering this relationship, make sure you are ready to be taken out of your comfort zone and into the realms of the unknown, because that's exactly where you will go. It's a wild ride and one that could bring out new or unknown aspects of yourself for all to see—even you. If you are presently in this relationship, apply the four Keys to the Kingdom, and let it rip.

The Keys to the Kingdom of the Jack of Clubs

Spontaneity

Spontaneity must become a natural impulse in order to keep up with the unconstrained energy of this card. You must be ready to *go* at any moment—ready to think differently, ready to change direction, and ready to wear a new hat of expression. The energy of this jack is excitable and lightning quick, so pay attention and respond with enthusiasm.

Think outside the Box

Creative thinking is a vital cornerstone of your communication. You must give your mind permission to think way beyond the boundaries of what is conventional, especially if you tend to like routines. It's crucial that you take action with your ideas as you share them with your partner, and these dynamics will keep the relationship exciting. Boredom, or *boring,* is not an option here. This will be like poison poured on the roots of a plant. Use the creative juice of this influence to generate newness in your relationship as well, as fresh energy is vital for your connection to thrive.

Change the World

One of the most meaningful aspects in the Jack of Clubs life path has to do with making a difference on a global scale. You do this by enhancing the quality of life for others in some way. Look at Oprah, who is a Jack of Clubs. I'm not suggesting that you try to match her efforts; however, do something to make a difference in someone else's life. This is the highest expression of this card's creative genius. Enjoy it in the biggest ways possible; even if what you do seems small to the eye, it could be gigantic to the heart of someone else.

Emotional Responsibility

Release the past, as there is no room for it here whatsoever! If emotional issues come up for you in this relationship, deal with them on your own, and do it quickly and efficiently. Do not take your emotional issues to your partner. Gain understanding and wisdom on your own, and then, rather than talking about it, live in the new behavior that is a result of your new self-understanding.

25
Queen *of* Clubs
Self-Awareness and Grace

T his card represents intuitive intelligence, mental organization, and self-awareness. As with all of the queens' natures, the underlying drive and innate nature of this card are to serve humanity in some way. Queens represent the receptive, spiritual nature of the human beings' experience on Earth. Clubs rule the mental realm, so this queen is focused on attitude and approaches, since whatever is received is relayed through the mind. Her intuitive and spiritual characteristics are expressed in balanced, wise, and logical ways. In the kingdom of relationship, this card takes things from the emotional realm to the realm of the mind, embracing reason and logic.

This influence will cause you to be drawn to those who have developed their intelligence and have a quick wit about them. You may have actually met your partner at a place or event that was related to intelligence and wit in some way, such as a library, a lecture, a comedy club, a workshop, or a service-oriented event of some kind. Service is actually a key to having a successful connection with this card— service and respect.

Respect is a big issue for this queen, so having her rule your relationship demands that there be no secrets kept; that communication be open, honest, and positive; and that honor and respect be expressed through actions and speech. Clear personal boundaries are necessary for maintaining clear thinking and good judgment. Jealousy and possessiveness must be locked away, and any tendencies toward arguing or confrontation must be turned into positive interaction and mutual support for one another. This queen embodies a restlessness that must be quenched. Travel to foreign lands, study, and explorations of people, spirituality, and anything that stimulates the mind are ways to answer her nature.

If you are presently in this relationship, know that sound reason, good conversation, and mental adventures are the highlights. Service to others puts you on the royal throne immediately. Express your appreciation for your partner and to your partner, so that he or she feels loved, wanted, and, most importantly, adored. This queen wants to feel adored, and both of you will want to feel this adoration, too. Be honest and maintain your mental balance by drawing on your logical mind rather than your emotions when communicating. Take the initiative to create adventure and movement in the relationship.

The Queen of Clubs is very sensitive and can be a bit nitpicky, even neurotic. Follow the suggestions listed within this compatibility description, as they can help to keep drama at bay. There can also be a dynamic within this connection that is a bit emotionally wishy-washy. It can show up like this

"I don't want to lose what I have, but maybe there is something else." This thinking is simply your creativity crying out for expression in some way. It will serve you to remember that dynamic and do something to express yourself, even if that action is just for fun. Independence is also a key issue with this card, so respect both yours and your partner's.

If you are looking at this relationship as a potential partnership, think carefully over what is being said and ask yourself if this is the type of relationship you would like to embark upon. Is it right for you? This connection can be a highly stimulating mental experience, and if you have a club birthday or have strong club influences in your life path, you will thrive in this relationship. You will also learn to refine your emotions and your self-expression, and perhaps you are unconsciously drawn to this relationship in order to do just that.

The Keys to the Kingdom of the Queen of Clubs

Respect

This queen has to be given respect, and respect for one another and for the relationship will be a major focus in your relationship. You must honor one another and respect each other's points of view, values, desires, and requests. You must listen with an open heart and open mind, and avoid intentionally challenging or confronting your partner. This journey is very much about refinement. The energy of this queen is gracious and intelligent in her expression, and as a couple, your expectations of one another are going to rise over time, requiring each of you to become more sensitive to the other's needs.

Adoration

Adoration is a key component for the Queen of Clubs. She loves to be adored and made to feel special, and this element will be prevalent in your connection together. Be demonstrative with your expressions of affection and appreciation, and this relationship will flourish like a beautiful garden.

Harmonious Environments

Beauty and harmony are required for balance and stability for each of you and the relationship itself. This card embodies an abundance of mental energy that is combined with heightened sensitivity; both need balance and harmony in the environment. When the external environment of your relationship is not harmonious, utter chaos will occur. Beauty, harmony, and peace will nurture both of you and your partnership, and they are imperative to this queen's sensitivity.

Independence

As much as this card loves attention, there is an absolute need for independence. Royal cards like to be in control. This element will be the nervous system of the relationship. Give one another the space to be the individuals that you are. If you are threatened when your partner is empowered, you have some work to do on yourself.

26

King *of* Clubs

The Power of Individuality

I t's quite possible that some sort of unusual encounter or unique situation brought the two of you together for your first meeting. Curious and eclectic, this connection is almost otherworldly when it comes to the way you will think and communicate with one another.

A King of Clubs relationship can be a wild and interesting ride, to say the least. The energy of this card is diverse, sometimes even bizarre. This king rules the mental realm of life and is strongly influenced by the planet Uranus, which transmits an unpredictable electric energy. So if you want to be in a relationship that is unconventional and exciting, you may have found the right one.

The King of Clubs is intended to be in partnership and thrives in relationship, which makes this an excellent composite for a couple. Together you will walk to the beat of your own drum, think outside the box, and give yourselves permission to do the relationship your way, rather than try to fit into society's or someone else's model of what a relationship is meant to be.

Marriage is blessed with this card, and the stronger and deeper the bond of love, the better. Home and family will be extremely important. Together, you will fashion a home that is eclectic and unique. You will love creating it together and sharing it with others. However, you might find that you have to guard against becoming reclusive, because with this connection it is all too easy to burrow away and forget the rest of the world.

The King of Clubs embodies a playful, creative spirit, which is vital to the happiness that will exist in the kingdom of your relationship. The only thing that could put a damper on the spirited expression of this influence would be getting stuck in ruts and routines. This will never do; it is totally unacceptable and must be avoided at all costs. If you see yourselves getting stuck, stimulate your minds and imaginations by sharing new ideas and generating new interests. This will reawaken the passionate spirit of this card. Communication is the lifeblood of this relationship and is the key to keeping things alive and healthy.

Working as partners or focusing on making money can bring great success, as good fortune is most often a given with this connection. Stepping into the limelight is an easy accomplishment for this king; if you desire being in the spotlight, so be it.

If you are in this relationship now, know that playfulness, sensuality, passion, communication, and the sharing of ideas are the elements that will keep love alive. If you are considering this relationship, know that you have to be up for the zany roller-coaster ride that it sometimes offers. If you prefer to be complacent in your life, this relationship may not be the place for you. However, it could be that you have drawn this connection to you so that you can come out of yourself in a new way and live a more extraordinary life in general. This relationship comes with a very powerful crown. As participants in this king's domain, you have the opportunity to wear the crown of passionate intelligence and creative expression. Recognize it, own it, and wear it with humble pride.

The only thing that could get in the way of this being a purely awesome relationship is if it's simply not happening at the right time according to the unfolding of your destinies. Remember, sometimes we connect with people we have known in other lifetimes—people who are our soul mates and people we travel with through eternity. Sometimes we touch each other for a moment in this life, feel the depth of our love for one another, and then move on because it's not the time to be together. If this relationship is not presently assigned to manifest as a partnership at this time, it most definitely has come to you to ignite your personal power of individuality.

The Keys to the Kingdom of the King of Clubs

Gratitude

The communication of gratitude is the foundation this connection must stand on. Your gratitude must be authentic, and you must be fully present in your delivery. If I were you, I would be very proactive in my expressions of gratefulness, because such outward displays are what will bring forth the greatness of this crown. Be real, be present, be honest, and be excited. Share all of your ideas and thoughts, and receive everything that your partner has to share with you—physically, mentally, emotionally, and spiritually.

Passion

Passion runs hot in the veins of this relationship connection, and it's something to be enjoyed in all its forms. This king will bring forth your passion and enhance your appreciation for and sensitivity to that which is beautiful and sensual. Allow this part of yourself to come alive in new ways, and most definitely express your appreciation for your partner openly and with enthusiasm.

Sensitivity to Beauty

The King of Clubs is tremendously sensitive to beauty and naturally gifted with a direct line to the source of creative intelligence. It is ever so important to express this brilliance in all arenas of your lives, both professional and personal. Support and inspire one another—always and in all ways.

Lightness of Heart

Playfulness and a lightness of heart are something that you want to keep present in the relationship. There is a childlike quality carried deep in the psyche of this great king, and it is more than worthy of your attention. So feed it with adventures of all kinds.

27
Ace of Diamonds
Ambition Fueled by Imagination

The unencumbered imagination of the Ace of Diamonds can inspire you to view your world from a brand new vantage point. Like all aces, this card is driven by desire. The Ace of Diamonds is a visionary. The natural ambition embodied within this influence is largely fueled by the imagination and visions of how the future could be. This card is blessed with unique perceptual abilities, and the enthusiasm with which they are expressed can be wildly influential over others. The driving forces of this ace are the possibilities it sees and a wish to bring those visions into the present.

On the mundane level of life, the desires for money and love are often the strongest motivations of this card, and this ambitious energy will be prevalent in this relationship. There will be no shortage of mental or physical energy with this connection in charge. Both of you will be launched like rockets into increased vitality, expanded thinking, and fresh ideas of how to make money.

The question of worth is at the forefront of the mind of this ace, and, for this reason, you will be expected to make your choices with clear intentions that align with your highest integrity. You and your partner will weave the question of value and worth into every decision that you consider. Diamonds question the value of everything, whether it's an item or person in their life. In this relationship, the Ace of Diamonds will encourage each of you to examine the value of things you have in your life, how you are using your time, and what you are doing for work. This card suggests that your honesty with one another is the most valuable asset you have. Without honesty, there will be disappointment and uncertainty.

Your being together sparks raw, creative, imaginative energy. This creative energy will need to be channeled in practical ways, otherwise things will become disjointed and lead to stress between the two of you. This abundance of creative intelligence will fill your minds with ideas. Put them into action. Work on projects together. Support one another to follow your dreams. The Ace of Diamonds is great at initiating anything having to do with making money. Whatever the nature of your relationship might be, it's likely that there's going to be a focus on money and a united drive to succeed with both in new and exciting ways. Also important to know is that this card initiates new personal values through its visionary approach to life. You will find that you each bring new ideas to the forefront—even in the way you do relationship.

Positive, honest, and direct communication is a key to making and keeping this relationship real and secure. Approaching this relationship with this self-awareness will create a solid foundation for the expression of your truest desires. Without the aforementioned foundation, things will become superficial and ultimately meaningless; you'll find yourselves going through the motions of being in the relationship, while feeling like something important is missing, and that will be true. If you find yourself feeling as if something is missing, dive more deeply into your connection with one another, be more authentic and present with each other, and communicate with clear, loving intentions. Physical displays of affection are very important for both of you to feel grounded and secure in the relationship.

There's an abundance of restlessness living in this connection, and you will need to keep life moving forward with focused intention so that you stay on track in practical, realistic ways. The ambitious nature of this ace embodies such vigor that it can easily take the driver's seat, leaving emotions in the dust. If you tend to be emotionally sensitive, or you have a strong need for emotional fulfillment, you might find this relationship a bit challenging. You can, however, become more emotionally independent in this relationship.

There can be a tendency to view this relationship through rose-colored glasses. Seeing reality as it really is will be most advantageous. To be in this partnership, you have to be at home in your own skin and comfortable in the relationship, and if that's not your experience, it may mean that you need to reevaluate the choices you're making. It could also mean that you could be more present with your awareness. Use the Keys to the Kingdom that follow, and learn how to remain in your personal power while being in partnership.

Having drawn this relationship your way suggests that you want to be more deeply in touch with what you truly desire. If your desires are clearly established in your heart and mind, but you feel that you cannot attain those desires in this relationship, it might be best to be in another situation. Only you know. This is very fast-moving energy that demands strength in individuality. If you're not getting what you need or want, there's only one person who can change that situation for you. To make that change, you might want to do a more in-depth examination of your relationship with yourself.

On the other hand, if you're in this relationship and enjoying this connection, including the ambitious drive and sometimes-unpredictable energy that come with it, good luck to you. This can be a really great connection. In the moments when you find it challenging, employ the suggestions being made and use the Keys to the Kingdom of the Ace of Diamonds to take your relationships to where you want it to be. There is always an invitation for growth present in an Ace of Diamonds relationship.

The Keys to the Kingdom of the Ace of Diamonds

Conscious Awareness

Conscious awareness is an important key for this relationship. Be present and listen actively and openly to what your partner is communicating. Be aware of his or her nonverbal signals, requests, and emotional needs. Listen to what is behind your partner's requests. Practice being receptive as you communicate; do this by listening while you are speaking. When you partner is speaking, listen from a place of stillness.

Create Security

Feeling secure and safe is vital for those in an Ace of Diamonds relationship. Trust and honesty are imperative for establishing emotional stability in this relationship. Show your vulnerability to one another, and keep your attitudes positive and your goals moving forward. Positive outlooks are essential, as negativity will pull the rug out from under your connection with one another.

Individuality

Be authentic and independent. This connection does not have room for codependence or needy behaviors. Strong self-esteem is needed, and if you don't have it, you will have the opportunity to develop it in this relationship. If you don't make the effort to do so, you will feel lost and insecure. Gather your strength from a place of authenticity, and you will grow strong in this relationship, both as an individual and together with your partner.

Shared Interests and Values

You must have and live by shared values in this relationship. Discuss what is important, and make an effort to express your values in unique ways as a couple. The stronger and more unified your values, the stronger and more unified your connection, and the healthier your relationship will be. Likewise, it's important for you and your partner to have shared interests and goals that you can pursue together. Action equals love for the Ace of Diamonds relationship.

28

Two *of* Diamonds

The Communication of Values

The Two of Diamonds oversees the communication of values by combining the elements of worth (values or money) with interaction. This card embodies the uniting energy of the two with the discriminating values of the diamond suit. The Two of Diamonds is blessed with the ability to access logic and intuition simultaneously, which gives it a highly evolved, skillful perception. This card suggests that we assign our intuition to the driver's seat and let our logic ride shotgun. The opportunities to learn how to balance logic and intuition will show up in this relationship. It's very simple, really: when you follow intuition, you will be guided in the best direction, and when you don't, you will run into obstacles.

Diamonds rule the realms of action, money, values, and worth. Being in this relationship can initiate strong concerns about or a focus on money, values, and what is right. This influence relates strongly to business as well, and it can motivate you to make things happen in regard to making money.

Under the influence of this card, you may notice that your personal will becomes more robust and perhaps aggressive. Communication in this relationship must be moderated with real emotion and feelings, as arguments are likely with this strong-willed deuce overseeing things. Actually, the Two of Diamonds enjoys a bit of arguing—it's like sparring or mental exercise. However, if this behavior is not kept in check, it will lead to the downfall of your relationship.

The secret of this relationship lies in making intuitive choices about the way you interact. The wisdom of this card suggests it is best to tune into your feeling self before opening your mouth. If you know that you're about to say something that doesn't feel quite right to say, don't say it! Intuition is the key that unlocks the door to the heart of this connection. The danger lurks in stubborn behaviors that govern how you think, in your ideas of how things should be, and in your need to be in control, if you have that. Displays of unconscious behaviors will lead directly to conflict and the demise of your connection. The opportunity here is to become more masterful with your mind. Train it. Master it rather than letting it master you. The need to engage in warlike behavior in an intimate relationship is the manifestation of old, unconscious patterns that stem from a lack of self-recognition and ownership of personal power. Simply see this behavior and change it in the moment it comes up.

There can also be struggles between love and money or between relationship and work, which come from the thinking that it's not possible to have both at the same time. These are real issues that the Two of Diamonds wrestles with. Recognize these issues when they arise, and learn to balance work and business with romance and play. It's definitely possible, however, the influences present with this card may need some convincing. It's all about choice. Working together or being in a mutual business can be very auspicious with this composite and will help to harmonize the struggle within this card regarding this issue of one or the other, work or relationship.

An opportunity that is present in this connection, which could be the very reason you have called it into your life, is to learn that having loyalty and understanding as a foundation in a relationship will build the strongest bond of love. If you cultivate these qualities, this can be an amazing connection for both of you. If you choose not to, you will be miserable.

Of course, there are always other factors. If you are in this relationship and it's a struggle for you, look first at how you love yourself and then how that self-love is reflected through your interaction with your partner. Your partner is reflecting back to you the relationship you have with yourself. Even though this dynamic happens in every relationship, it's more profoundly present in two-governed relationships than in others. This dynamic is exactly what a two relationship is all about—communication begins within and is reflected without. That's the bottom line. So, essentially, you have brought someone into your life who will mirror your essence, your expression, your thinking, and your subconscious mind. Take care to see what you're actually looking at and develop your independence and self-expression from a place of self-understanding and awareness. Commitment to what is real will empower you to do this. And it will have an amazing effect on your connection with your partner and how you show up in your life.

If you're presently in this relationship and it's a struggle, apply the wisdom that is being offered here to bring the relationship into its fullest potential. The relationship must thrive, not just survive. This particular connection takes more effort than some because of this card's robust nature. However, it can be a remarkable relationship if you do it right.

If you're considering this relationship as a possibility for yourself, know that the person you are uniting with will be a mirror in which you will see everything about yourself. The perceptual abilities of the Two of Diamonds are exquisite and unwavering, and within them lies the power to enhance your perception and your communication skills through the transformation you will go through in this relationship.

The Keys to the Kingdom of the Two of Diamonds

Intuition versus Logic

Intuition is your very best friend here. It's so easy for this card to be overrun with reason and rationale, which undeniably leads straight to conflict. Individually and as a couple, you must learn to follow your intuition and avoid letting logic and the rational mind make choices for you. Be with your feelings and follow them, as they will lead you in the right direction. Give logic the job of supporting your intuition.

Introspection

The passion inherent in this card can really stir up deep emotions. Introspection will help you avoid engaging in old, unconscious emotional patterns from past relationships. Turn within to explore and discover any sabotaging thoughts that lead to destructive behaviors. Use introspection as a tool of transformation and self-empowerment.

Communication

How you communicate is unbelievably important in your relating with one another. You must be honest, open, authentic, and constant. Twos love to talk. They have to talk. It is how they connect themselves to the world around them. If communication falls into the shadows, your connection will be lost.

Honesty and Vulnerability

Remember that this connection is based in values, so honesty is a must. If you create the space for anything other than integrity, that thing will manifest. Be forthright, truthful, and vulnerable. When you choose to do so, the ingenious mind inherent in this connection will express itself through you in ways that are unsurpassed.

29

Three of Diamonds

From Rags to Riches

It's likely that you felt the hands of fate or destiny at work in bringing this relationship into being. This is someone who is a soul mate to you. This soul-mate connection doesn't always mean that you're meant to be together for an extended period of time, or at all; that could be true as well, but it's not for certain. This maybe–maybe not dynamic is exactly the energy of a three relationship.

The fact that you've found each other, however, does mean that you have something to complete together, something to learn from one another, and the opportunity for character development. It also means that you have something very special to give to one another, and there can be magic for each of you in discovering what that is. On the high side of things, there will be tremendous passion in this relationship and a deep and powerful connection of the heart. Keeping that passion alive can be just a bit tricky at times.

Avoid getting stuck in ruts and routines with each other and with life in general. This is not the kind of relationship that does well with traditional concepts. That doesn't mean you can't live together or get married—it just means that the relationship has to be lived with its own unique expressions. You will have to put a new slant on the traditional aspects of your relationship, because the relationship's expression could change on a pretty consistent basis. Devoid of freedom of expression and out-of-the-box thinking, this connection will spiral downward quickly and become stressful and disempowering for both of you. The Three of Diamonds relationship has to be lived like a love affair. That could be fun!

Personal sacrifice and denial of your best self could be challenges that arise with this connection. Being in this relationship can bring about money worries as well. This is a very creative card, actually, but it is one of the most difficult life paths in the deck when it comes to relationships. Self-sacrifice, worry, and struggle are bound to be familiar experiences unless you tap into the creative genius that this card embodies. The Three of Diamonds is known as the card of financial creativity; however, its creative intelligence can be applied to all forms of expression. Use the unlimited imagination of this card to put goals and projects into action, and you will transform the challenging aspects of this card into a bounty of good fortune and happiness.

It's likely that you've attracted this relationship to learn unconditional love and self-acceptance, and to let go of old fears regarding your place in life—where you belong, if you belong, and so on. Transforming your doubt into self-love will give you the confidence you need to dive deeply into the intimate connection that you truly desire; however, you must first let go of your fears. Face them head on and see them for what they are—old stories that have no place in this relationship. Use the Keys to the Kingdom to enliven your connection and make your relationship an artistic adventure, a journey of discovery of both yourself and your partner. Real gratitude will be the magic carpet that carries you into the abundance that this relationship connection has to offer.

If you're in this relationship and you're finding it to be a challenge, be honest and ask yourself if you are in the right place. If you're committed to making things work, use the Keys to the Kingdom to enhance your communication and see what happens. You will have to apply the keys on a consistent basis. It does take commitment to be in this relationship. You can't make an effort once and then expect things to be fine.

If you are considering this relationship, read carefully, *feel,* and think about your personal experience of being with this person relative to what's being said here. Often we meet people and are drawn to them because we have been with them in the past or because they have shown up to reflect something back to us. This can be that kind of relationship. Just take the time to be clear about what is motivating you to make the decisions and choices that you are drawn to make. If you have a three as your birth card, or were born on a three day in the month (meaning the 3rd, 12th, 21st, or 30th of the month) this can be a great connection for you.

The Keys to the Kingdom of the Three of Diamonds

Self-Confidence

This connection can bring up self-doubt that lives deep in the belly of the subconscious mind, and it will also test your beliefs in regard to your "belonging" in life. These experiences, if they come up for you, will be opportunities to let go of old stories that have nothing to do with who you really are. When you take such a journey with yourself, you will initiate the power of your authenticity, which is most certainly a must for communication with your partner to be real. Superficiality or game-playing will diminish this connection in a heartbeat. It's vital that, as an individual, you be forthright and just with all of your actions, and you can only do that from a place of self-confidence.

Choose Creativity

When worries or fears poke their little heads into your experience, realize that they are actually creative energy that is not being channeled. When creativity is not put to use, it shows up in forms of restlessness, which, if ignored, then turn into uncertainty, worries, and fear. When these unconstructive experiences are present, know that you have a tremendous resource of creative intelligence knocking at the door of your mind. And this particular brand of creative genius is brilliant at making money. Choose creativity over lack!

Deepen Your Trust

The Three of Diamonds can feel as though it's not always sure where it is, and this influence will certainly visit each of you from time to time. If you or your partner has trust issues, they will rise to the surface for your review. It's a perfect environment to cultivate confidence in yourself, your experience, and your perception, not to mention in your comfort with and expression of intimacy.

Self-Expression

Self-expression is of major importance in this relationship. This is a card of creative expression, and, as an individual, you must engage in your own, unique expression of self. In addition, you must give yourself permission to be all that you are, in all the ways you want to be. Clear emotional boundaries will support each of you in doing so. The more uniquely authentic your expression is, the better, so don't be afraid to tap into the unusual or that which is totally new and different.

30

Four *of* Diamonds

Seeing through the Veil

Upon entering this relationship you might find yourself asking, "Is this a fantasy or is it reality?" or perhaps, "Is this my dream come true?" This connection may very well feel like the latter and at the same time be a total fantasy, so you must consult your intuition and call forth your discernment abilities to determine if you are projecting a fantasy into being or not. What I mean by *projecting* is that often times the Four of Diamonds would rather be in a less-than-perfect relationship than be alone. When this choice is made, the relationship is often perceived differently by each of the parties; each one of you has totally different intentions, goals, and perceptions regarding what kind of relationship you are actually in. This discrepancy is often present with a Four of Diamonds relationship connection.

Another trait in this card's character is the more practical expression of its nature, where you will find the path to good fortune, a comfortable home life, and possible adventures at sea. You will be happiest when romance, adventure, and practicality form a triangle of perfection as a result of how you choose to relate and live with one another. This card has a very juicy side to it as well, and the nature of the beast must be fed.

The Four of Diamonds is known to guarantee financial protection and security, so unless you are totally irresponsible with your money, this arena of life should be good. This card encourages greater focus in regard to work and productivity, and each of you will have an enhanced awareness of creating and maintaining stability, consistency, and structure. The Four of Diamonds also blesses you with an abundance of creative intelligence, and you are likely to have the desire to advance in some way in your life. This desire could lead you to pursue new interests, go back to school, or get additional training in your present field of interest.

Though fours are associated with structure, the essence of this card is adventurous, playful, and loves change. The sometimes-fickle temperament of this card can lead to feelings of uncertainty when your communication is challenged or blocked. When this happens, you have to be open and receptive and remain true to your highest personal values, as this will bring clarity to your thinking and your communication. Nothing less will do. Clarity of your values and emotional discernment are key; they must be what you live by, because when these elements are in place, this relationship becomes fulfilling and fantastic.

It's common for the Four of Diamonds to be less expressive with emotions, and this reticence could show up in your relating. At times it can seem that you take each other and the relationship for granted, so it's wise to take time and consciously make the effort to express your feelings and emotions. It will be essential for your partner to hear, feel, and see your love for him or her, and it will be essential for you to see evidence of his or her love as well. Honesty needs to be a given in order for your relationship to thrive. Not so much as a little white lie should enter the sacred domain of this relationship, as it will undermine everything that has been worked for.

If you are in this relationship and things seem challenging, perhaps both of you need to be more expressive with your affection, emotions, and feelings. If your partner is gone for a day and you miss her, tell her. If you like the way he looks, tell him. Speak what is on your mind. If something is bothering you, explore it in your own self first to gain clarity and understanding, and then, if appropriate, share it with your partner.

You may have brought this relationship to yourself to learn to be more expressive with your affections and feelings. Take care to avoid hiding behind work and getting caught up in being overly busy. Initiate time to play and explore together, as these are the very activities that will make this relationship successful.

The Keys to the Kingdom of the Four of Diamonds

Expressions of Affection

Show your partner affection and express your feelings, because these are the keys that will keep your relationship alive and juicy. Remember to let your partner know, in every way, that you love him or her. Buy her flowers, do special little things for him from time to time (with not too much time in between), speak your feelings, and be physically affectionate. All of these acts compose a language all its own, a way of communicating that is vital for this to be a happy relationship.

Variety

Even though the Four of Diamonds is a structured influence, its spirit (inner essence) card is the Five of Spades, which is a card of change that loves variety. Adventure must be on the list of things to do. Explore activities that support the dreamy side of this card, such as being on or near the water.

Open Communication

Take time to have meaningful conversations on a regular basis. It's way too easy, with this connection, to become taskmasters and get stuck in a rut of not communicating about what's important. Failing to spend quality time together will deteriorate the delicate fiber of this relationship.

Honor Your Principles

Having shared values is the key to your connection's longevity. The Four of Diamonds carries an innate responsibility to higher values. This means that integrity and trustworthiness must prevail and that each of you must choose to be responsible with your words and deeds.

31

Five of Diamonds

Seeking the Truth

The Five of Diamonds is commonly known as the seeker of truth. The influences of this card lead us to change our values through the search to find the deeper meaning in and true value of the things in our lives. Through these experiences, we expand our awareness and change our values to encompass the world in a bigger, more impersonal way.

As a relationship ruler, this card infuses a creative and somewhat futuristic type of mentality into the partnership and into you as individuals. By *futuristic,* I mean that this influence tends to use intelligence to understand emotions and feelings, rather than allowing you to fall into emotional black holes of misunderstanding that lead directly to chaos and drama. The Five of Diamonds loves freedom, and a Five of Diamonds relationship must have tangible components of personal freedom, exploration and adventure, and change and variety for it to thrive and live long. Intelligence and intuition are the strong governing elements that guide the way for each of you and your relationship. One of the most powerful things that can be learned in this relationship is how to consciously use the power of one-on-one communication to create harmony.

Don't expect this relationship to unfold like a romantic novel. It won't. It will, however, have its own brand of magic, and with it comes a new way of seeing, time and time again. The energy of this card is fresh, distinctive, and different. It will bring you new experiences to explore and learn from on a regular basis. There's a childlike quality about the Five of Diamonds that may awaken your curiosity and innocence and give you new eyes with which to view life.

Socializing, being with friends and family, and spending time with groups will be important and will most likely occupy a fair amount of your time together. People will be drawn to your energy and want to engage with you. The combination of fortunate blessings and popularity could put you in the limelight and bring you success. You and your partner could actually create lucrative business situations for yourself. The Five of Diamonds has abundant creative energy to draw from to make things happen. The key to generating personal success in this relationship lies in making the choice to be adaptable, reliable, and focused. Daily exercise or physical activities of some sort help harness the fast-moving mental energy of this card and bring it into focus. Secrets and lies are totally unacceptable. Keep communication open and forthright. Otherwise, the very fabric of the relationship will be undermined and eventually destroyed.

Spiritual discipline or a disciplined practice of some sort is suggested with this card and will support your relationship. The study of history, religion, spirituality, or the ancient mysteries of life might become interesting to you. Together you could uncover some old secrets having to do with humanity, your families, yourself, or each other. Let your curiosity lead the way.

If you are in this relationship and experiencing challenges of some kind, take to heart what is being said here and implement the Keys to the Kingdom. It's likely that in doing so you can turn things to how you would like them to be.

Don't project your fears onto your partner. Projecting fears into the relationship can be a pattern for some with this card as a composite, and the fear is probably something from your past. If you find that your thoughts and statements often begin with *you*—as in, "You always do . . ." or "You never . . ."—then you are projecting your stuff onto your partner. Stop yourself, and take an account of what you can do to change the behavior within yourself.

This relationship is all about experience. The energy of the five wants to gather experiences and, in turn, share them with the rest of the world. That seeking-and-sharing aspect of the card can make this a fantastic connection. However, if you don't have an innate curiosity and a desire to know what makes the world go round, then you either need to wake up the child within or find a relationship that is more aligned with who you really are.

If you are considering this relationship as a possibility for yourself, be sure that you resonate with what is being said. The influences that are present in a relationship composite will always be present in the partnership. You can grow from and with them, or you can struggle. It's a choice. This is a card of change, and changes will be a constant in one form or another. Making the right choice for yourself as an individual before you enter a relationship can make all the difference in your journey in life and in the relationships you have now and in the future. This particular relationship can awaken the innocent curiosity within the mind of an adult. It's a blessing that is full of surprises and the unknown, and it will bless you with the freedom to be who you want to be.

The Keys to the Kingdom of the Five of Diamonds

Selfless Acts of Giving

This relationship path suggests that giving to others in a way that enhances the quality of their lives will return great rewards, bring wonderful self-fulfillment, and yield many unexpected blessings. This will be true for the two of you as a team and for each of you personally. Giving to one another is equally important. Giving first, without expectations of receiving, will create a strong bond of love and trust.

Mental Discipline

Fives are not designed to accomplish. They are designed to seek new experiences. Therefore, the energy of this card is constantly moving outward in a variety of directions concurrently. That's its nature: to seek and find. This dynamic can create scattered mental energy for you and make it difficult for you to focus on goals, projects, and even the day-to-day things that need to be handled. Physical activity on a daily basis will help harness this energy and support you in directing it.

Connecting with Innocence

Your connection with one another is the master weaver of the fabric of this relationship. The communication between you must be open, honest, and loving at all times. If something is bothering you, work it out with yourself first and then decide whether or not it's necessary to talk about it. Take responsibility for your verbal actions in this relationship, and remember that emotional drama does not fare well here. The energy of this relationship is already full of movement from the five. Adding drama makes things shaky and chaotic, and then time is needed for recovery. Be with the innocent nature of this card and let it permeate your relationship.

Personal Freedom

Give one another permission to be free in your self-expression, without expectation and without judgment. I am not suggesting an open relationship, where you are running around dating other people, unless that's your agreement. I am suggesting that you honor and respect one another as the individuals you are, and support each other in being yourselves as individuals in the most fulfilling ways possible. Know and honor the fact that you will each need your own time to be and play in individual arenas. Any fear or insecurity that comes up around individual personal freedom needs to be dealt with and altered into maturity.

32

Six of Diamonds

Responsibility to Values

Six-based relationships are often a reunion of some sort, from either this lifetime or another, and it is more than likely that the hand of fate brought the two of you together this time. The question might be, why?

This card represents responsibility to higher values, and what you value will be the key component to making this connection work, or not. Integrity to self and one another has to be the very foundation that this relationship stands on, or it will not stand at all.

Sharing and talking are the magic elements to making this a great working relationship. You will have to remind yourself—and perhaps each other—not to take things too seriously, as doing so can lead to the development of difficult or fixed behaviors in your communication. This is a strong-willed card, and there will be times when you butt heads, debate your opinions, and simply want to spar a bit with language and your minds. These things can be good fun, as long as that's how you perceive them. The secret lies in your ability to maintain your senses of humor. If you take things too personally, or yourselves too seriously, the fun can quickly turn into ego battles and power struggles, which can be hard to recover from.

Physical activity is vital for this relationship to be healthy. In fact, just being part of this connection can actually cause you to be more physical in your life, and this Six of Diamonds energy definitely has the power to make your body stronger. Engage in activities and adventures that involve physical movement. This card has a highly charged sexual influence as well, and you might have to guard against overindulgence in this area; physical, mental, and emotional balance are the keys to keeping things clear and moving forward in positive directions. Enjoy the fabulous chemistry, while keeping things in balance at the same time.

Emotions can waver quite frequently with this relationship connection, so you must learn to become like a river and go with the flow of your feelings, attending to them yourself to gain clarity before sharing them with your partner. The personal will becomes stronger with this card, and it's important to give way rather than push your partner with your opinions.

Success will come to you when you focus your attention elsewhere other than on your personal desires—meaning, if you chase money, it will run away, or if you crave attention, people will ignore you. The better choice is to align your intention with plans for how you can improve the quality of someone else's life, as this way of thinking and being creates a magnetic force of good fortune for everyone. This doesn't mean that you don't have your own financial goals—you absolutely do. However, you have to choose balance in your approach to life. The Six of Diamonds demands that you take responsibility for the change you see is needed. This influence will create the need to make adjustments or compromises from time to time in regard to relationships, communication, or finances. This card will also demand responsibility to financial commitments and the law, so if such things in your life are incomplete, overdue, or have simply been ignored, you will be called to the table to deal with them. Social gatherings, personal and professional connections, and networking with groups bring the greatest avenues for material gain and good standing. Network and be with others often.

As the Six of Diamonds is a highly intuitive card, intuition will play a major role in your decision-making, and you should always follow what your gut is telling you. You can trust that your intuitive hits are right on when you are clearly connected to your inner awareness.

Personal will in each of you will be stronger with this connection, so you must know that there is a potential for power struggles and head-to-head combat, so to speak. The learning opportunities of this card encourage and develop greater self-understanding. You will have many opportunities to choose being more lighthearted and less fixed. Higher values, above and beyond all else, will have to be the primary foundation of your being together. Passion is a given with this connection.

If you are considering this relationship, ask yourself if these possibilities excite you. If you are presently in this relationship, remember to keep things moving with physical activities, great communication, and new adventures in your thinking. This card is extremely physical, and your connection will thrive on these kinds of activities. It's also a social card, and getting together with others and sharing interests will strengthen the bond between you. If you seem to be caught in repeated battles of the will and ego, use the keys that follow to create a different way of relating and then see what happens. You have the power to make the difference. Use it!

The Keys to the Kingdom of the Six of Diamonds

Responsibility

The Six of Diamonds carries a responsibility to integrity. This influence will demand that you be responsible for your interactions in your relationships, your finances, any legal dealings that come your way, and the way you communicate with others. If you fail to be in integrity in some area of your life, the influences at work here will make that known by putting obstacles in your way. For most people, this is not a problem, but if you have the habit of letting things slide rather than taking care of them, that will have to change in this relationship. It's best to be proactive.

Physical Activity

The Six of Diamonds is a card of physical strength and endurance. Many world-class athletes have Six of Diamonds birthdays. This physical energy must be channeled in some way, or it will build up and turn into tension, which then often results in conflict. You can use physical activity to diffuse tension between you. It's very effective.

Kindness and Patience

The Six of Diamonds can be a very willful, hard-driving energy. On one hand, it's a very sexy and playful, generous, sweet energy. On the other, it can be "my way or the highway," unyielding and intolerant. All of these characteristics will manifest in your relationship from time to time. It's so important to be kind to and patient with one another.

Adventurous Play

There is a playful, childlike quality to this card that needs to be acknowledged and supported. This particular characteristic is going to inspire the innocence in your connection, so it's very important. Take time to do simple, playful things together. Make time to socialize with other as well, as it will be important for you to have lots of people in your life.

33

Seven of Diamonds

Heaven Meets Earth

The Seven of Diamonds symbolizes the union of spirit and matter, the union of spiritual and material values, and the union of heaven and earth. The energy of this card encourages refinement and sensitivity in all areas of life. Family, home, relationships, and money will be significantly affected in valuable ways with this relationship connection. Additionally, there will be great importance placed on education and the gathering of information.

With time, this can be a deeply rewarding relationship; however, there may be hurdles to jump along the way, as bringing heaven and earth together is not an easy task. Sweetness and affection are the keys to keeping things alive, on track, and juicy. Passion is a featured component of this relationship, and passion is going to rouse your emotions in very deep ways. This stirring of emotion can cause uncertainty. The best way to move through challenging, emotional times is to talk about them as they are happening. Use your rational mind when engaging in these conversations rather than spewing emotional confusion. Emotional drama will spiral the two of you into hell when you're aiming for heaven.

Give to one another, as expressions of gratitude for what you have together will be the greatest source of your strength. At the heart of the Seven of Diamonds is a pure and innocent love that knows only of giving, sometimes to a fault. Your friendship will be the very foundation of your oneness, so make it your first priority. Be your own best friend first, and then be best friends with your partner. It is through your connecting in this way that the strongest bond of love will be formed, grow, and thrive.

Money and finances can be the major issues, and these issues are often based in fear. The Seven of Diamonds says, "Let go of your fears around money and have faith." That doesn't mean that you just sit around and do nothing to secure your finances. It does mean that you must unify your spiritual and material beliefs, and take action to do what makes you happy and brings you success. When money issues come up, they must be dealt with in practical ways. This card is actually known as the millionaires' card. In order to access the greatest earthly rewards of this influence, negative beliefs around money must be obliterated to give way to new positive beliefs. Use old fears as a platform for new perspectives that take you outside old paradigms and into new empowerment.

If you are in this relationship now, know that the secret to its success will be found in your friendship together and your expression of love for one another. Let go of fears, or work through them together by communicating deeply about what's really going on. Find the root of the challenge and remove it. Explore new possibilities together, and find ways to give to others. Self-awareness plays a strong role in this card's life path, and it will be advantageous to have spirituality as a mainstay in your relationship as well.

If you are considering going into this relationship, know that it will demand that you refine your beliefs and goals, let go of your fears, and give more than you receive. This relationship can grow into one that is very special, as long as you both rise to the occasion and step up to the plate to give of yourself 100 percent.

If you're presently in this relationship and find yourself dealing with challenges, apply the wisdom of the cards to extract the beauty of this relationship, and give way to its magic. This is a place where your heart will be opened wide for you to experience self-love in a greater way than ever before.

The Keys to the Kingdom of the Seven of Diamonds

Refinement

In this relationship, you will be encouraged to refine your beliefs about who you are and how you love. You will refine your way of being in relationship with yourself and with another. You will refine your values regarding what is most important to you. And you will refine your relationship with money. Every one of these categories of living is up for review and has the opportunity be reconstructed in the best ways possible.

Friendship

The key to establishing and maintaining trust at the foundation of this connection is friendship. Always be a friend to yourself first and then a friend to your partner. This card knows how to do friendship better than any other in the deck. Take advantage of this wisdom, apply it in your relationship, and reap the benefits that only this card can give you regarding the care and maintenance of the human heart.

Trust What You Know

This is huge in this relationship and something worth giving yourself to. Each time we choose to have faith, trusting what we innately know is true, and take the steps that accompany our knowing, we empower ourselves greatly. Not only do we empower ourselves, but we also empower those around us to do the same. Learning to trust your inner knowing is a genuine opportunity with this connection. The wisdom you gain from learning to trust yourself will be more than valuable for you and for your connection with your partner.

Unconditional Love and Acceptance

These are most valuable keys for making this relationship all it can be. This card teaches us to forgive and to accept things as they are. By doing so, we free others and ourselves from judgment. Forgiveness is perhaps the most powerful action we can take to allow true love to heal the past, the present, and the future.

34

Eight of Diamonds

Being in the Limelight

Are you ready to be in the spotlight? If the answer is yes, then perhaps you have come to the right place. When this connection occurs, your partnership may go on stage for the entire world to see. It might not be seen by the entire world; however, there's a very good chance that, at least in your inner circles, your friends and family will always have great interest in what's going on with you and your relationship.

The Eight of Diamonds has a strong, energetic spirit. It definitely wants things its way. The willful energy of this card can manifest in the form of ego battles and power struggles between the two of you. These interactions are likely to turn into emotional drama. In these moments it will be wise of you to remember the importance that your relationship holds for you, so that you can become clear in your thinking. Making this choice will help you keep things in perspective. When you channel this powerful, creative energy with openness and receptivity, there will be no limits to what you can achieve for yourselves. The best way to redirect this aggressive energy is to deepen your connection with one another through acknowledgment and mutual support, rather than being competitive with one another. Keeping this aggressive energy in check is something you're going to have to stay on top of in this relationship. If you don't, it will be all too easy to become judgmental, thinking that you know what is best for your partner, and your partner will do the same with you. If you aren't careful, superiority competitions will bring this relationship to its knees. Keep your eyes open for this type of behavior in yourself so that you can nip it in the bud.

Keep your spiritual and material values in alignment and make both of them a priority. You'll have to let go of old, subconscious ways of thinking that cause indecisiveness or uncertainty. Uncertainty and doubt are flags waving in your face to tell you that you need to apply your creative self and express who you are to the world. Otherwise, this unacknowledged creative energy will turn sour and show up in the relationship through power struggles.

The Eight of Diamonds is a highly creative card. It embodies unlimited potential and natural talent. Being in this relationship will evoke those attributes of your personalities, and it's important that each of you find avenues to express your creativity. Self-discipline is key to maintaining your emotional balance. There is an abundance of personal power embodied in this card. The application of discipline, whether it be through meditation, martial arts, yoga, or study of some kind, is essential to this connection.

If you are presently in this relationship, beware of and guard against power struggles, as they are certain to undermine your connection with one another. Create together, honor one another, and support each other. Be spontaneous, have adventures, and produce together. This is a very powerful connection, and if you are willing to let go of past fears and draw on the higher, most positive expression of the Eight of Diamonds, you can achieve absolutely anything that you strive for. Ask yourself what you bring to the table and acknowledge that. Look to see and acknowledge what your partner brings to the table and acknowledge that. You must join as equals—across the board.

If you're not yet in this relationship but considering it as a possibility, be sure it's the kind of relationship you are looking for. This partnership will be on stage and in the limelight. It's high powered and dynamic. There will be drama and raw power to deal with; on the high side of things, this connection will empower and liberate you to express your personal genius. You only have to be willing to relinquish your need to be in control and learn to be open and receptive to the goodness that wants to come your way. Worry and fear will not work here. Working in partnership will. You'll have the opportunity to be a team player while maintaining your individuality. It could be that you have drawn this person to yourself, or are drawn to him or her, to learn to assume your personal power in a greater way and to learn how to be in a relationship where both parties support one another equally to be all they can be.

The Keys to the Kingdom of the Eight of Diamonds

Self-Discipline

This relationship connection provides a tremendous opportunity to cultivate self-awareness through self-discipline. Being in this relationship will infuse you with great power to express yourself. It will also ignite your will and need to be in control. Your greatest opportunity, in these respects, is to learn greater self-discipline. The essence of the Eight of Diamonds is represented by self-mastery. Self-mastery over your mind and emotions will serve you more greatly than anything else, in all arenas of your life.

Acknowledgment and Support

You must, first and foremost, above and beyond all else, acknowledge and support each other to be all that you can be. There can be a tendency for one-upmanship with this card—the "I can do it better than you" syndrome. Don't go there. Each time you acknowledge your partner, it paves the way for your own acknowledgment, which, by the way, is the key to you being able to acknowledge another. You must first genuinely acknowledge yourself—who you are, what your talents are, and what you bring to the table of this relationship. When you truly own your greatness, you empower your partner to do the same.

Creative Expression

Creativity is a given with this connection, and it's important for each of you to establish avenues for expressing your innate gifts. Your avenues of expression will range from simplicity to complexity—from decorating the house together to performing on stage or getting involved in political issues. Cultivate and maintain your independence and unique brand of self-expression and engage with your partner as well. Give yourself permission to do everything you want to do in the best ways possible. Just be sure that, in some way, you're manifesting the creative intelligence that's an integral part of this card's life path.

The Use of Will

How you choose to use your personal will will be of major importance and will determine the outcomes that you create for yourselves and your relationship. For this reason, you must cultivate your discernment and right use of will, and thus know when to stand strong and when to yield.

35

Nine of Diamonds

The Opportunity to Give

This won't be a traditional type of relationship. The nature of the Nine of Diamonds is universal, eclectic, and meant to be exciting, and these qualities will also apply to this relationship. The magnetic energy of this composite has to be harnessed and directed for you to reap the benefits it has to offer, and it's through your interactions with one another that you will capture it. Communication is a very big deal in this relationship, and you're going to want to talk about anything and everything. You will want to share everything with each other. In doing so, remember to maintain your sense of self rather than getting lost in your partner and later coming around to the fact that you left yourself behind somewhere. Your individuality must have good boundaries at all times.

Avoid getting stuck in mundane routines, because when boredom strikes, the relationship will suffer. If you notice that the mundane aspects of life are taking over, initiate interaction with the world around you. The nature of the Nine of Diamonds is to share its knowledge through interaction, networking, and promotion. In fact, having this as a relationship connection can spark interest in careers involving these types of activities, and these types of careers could lead to satisfaction and success.

Nine-governed relationships embody opportunities to let go of behaviors, ideas, and values that no longer serve us. Remain aware in those moments when life gives you an opportunity to let go of something that you no longer need or that no longer has anything to do with who you are now. Hanging on to the past will cause pain and frustration. Letting go of old fears surrounding the intimacy of love is the real opportunity with this connection, and it will be best to take advantage of that opportunity when it arises.

Hold onto your wallet! This card loves to shop, spend money, and indulge in the finer things in life. At the same time, this connection can support a great business partnership. This will be most especially true if your focus is enhancing others' quality of life by empowering them to become greater. Your relationship will flourish as much as or even more than those you touch and empower. Working together is favored, and you will reap the greatest rewards by doing meaningful things for others.

If you're presently in this relationship, you have a golden opportunity to harness this amazing energy and focus it in the directions of your choosing. There can be elements of surprise evoked by this card, so expect the unexpected along the way. The two of you and your relationship will thrive when you live outside the realms of what is conventional. Live a life that is eclectic, original, and free from the expectations of others. If you're feeling stuck, get out and do something. Being stuck is a result of not taking decisive action. Action changes everything, and *action* is the key word for the diamond suit.

If you're considering this relationship, don't try reading between the lines here. The essence of the Nine of Diamonds is a universal energy. It moves personal issues to the surface and out of the picture—unless, of course, you choose to hold onto them, which simply causes misery. Read carefully and be clear on whether or not this is the type of relationship you desire. If you want to have babies and live the American dream, this relationship may not get you there. I'm not saying it's impossible, but it's not as probable as it is with some other composite cards. If you do choose to live a traditional type of life, you will have to have your own brand of tradition, and you will have to do everything your own way rather than bending to the expectations of others.

The Keys to the Kingdom of the Nine of Diamonds

Individuality and Co-creation

Your individuality is where your strength will be found. Strength is given to the relationship when each of you contributes your personal signature of self-expression. Co-creation will keep your relationship thriving. Embrace yourself and proudly share yourself with your partner—and support one another in doing this.

Giving to Others

Once you have authenticated your individual strengths and the strength of your partnership, begin making the world a better place by enhancing the lives of other people. Investing your time in such efforts will yield the greatest returns imaginable.

Be Unique

Living an eclectic lifestyle and giving yourselves the freedom to explore and discover new and different ways of being in a relationship will not only make you happy and deepen your bond of love, but it will give others permission to do the same for themselves. See yourselves as pioneers in this way. The Nine of Diamonds, remember, is a networking promoter of ideas. Together you can give the world new models for living in larger spheres of expression.

Take Action

Physical movement and intentional action will ensure success, both personally and professionally. Mundane existence can become boring for the Nine of Diamonds energy. It is happiest when life is on the move, and you will be also. Don't let life become a routine, because routine will strangle your relationship. Keep life alive and moving forward at all times. Create, initiate, and enjoy!

36

Ten of Diamonds

Fortunate Blessings

Known as the blessed card, the Ten of Diamonds bestows this relationship with great good fortune and endless opportunities. It's easy to assume that your initial encounter was destined to happen, and it's likely to lead to good luck and good fortune. This is one of the most blessed financial unions in the deck; whether abundance comes from inheritance, from something you create together, or from winning the lottery, it is meant to be, and it is a gift from life to the two of you.

There is a catch, though: the Ten of Diamonds asks that you express your gratitude for the gifts you're going to receive *before* you get them, and you do this by making the effort to get what it is that you want. You have to work hard. You will always be taken care of and blessed with good fortune in all areas of life; you just have to make diligent efforts to manifest your desires.

It will be auspicious for you to be involved in community activities, volunteer work, or anything that is service oriented. These types of efforts will help you achieve, maintain, and grow your good fortune. These actions, of course, have to be taken from the heart, not for the gain. Your intention must be of the highest integrity, as the diamond suit rules not only money, but also values. So keep your values high and your intentions clear, and you will keep yourselves in good standing with the generosity of life itself.

Social life and family will be at the top of the priority list in this relationship and will be a constant focus of your time. There is tremendous drive and ambition, creativity, and passion in this connection, and keeping things focused can sometimes be a challenge. When you employ mental discipline and single-mindedness, whatever you put your effort toward will bring rewards; you will have to work to get there, though, as hard work is part of the deal. Your good fortune will always come quickly when you are caring about others—humans, animals, or the environment. The right use of your will is the bottom line in this agreement with life. If you choose to live a selfish, unaware existence, all of this great good fortune could be wasted on gambling and overindulgence, or on pure selfishness. That's not what the crown of this connection wants for you. At the heart of this connection, there is a call to serve humanity. Heed that call, and the mother of life will bless you beyond your wildest dreams.

Any uncertainty or emotional insecurity experienced by either of you is most likely the result of emotional restlessness and can be alleviated with creative expression, physical activities, or better communication. The Ten of Diamonds has selfish tendencies that can lead to being a bit self-absorbed, so it's important to make listening to your partner a priority. Explore your deepest self and let go of old selfish behaviors, if you have them. This is a blessed relationship. Take advantage of its blessings and then shine like a diamond to light the world around you. This card is romantic. Indulge in the romance and the perpetual renewing of your love.

There are, of course, challenges, which with this card seem more like tests. The land mines that could blow up in your face will be planted by selfish attitudes and behaviors that cause you to focus on what you think you're not getting, rather than on what you have and what you can give. Be careful where you put your attention. Gratitude is the key.

If you're in this relationship now, please know that riding the higher aspects of this card's path is the best way to go. When you are aligned with your integrity and express your gratitude by giving back to life in some way, this is an awesome connection that will bring blessings of great good fortune again and again. If you are being frivolous with your intention and not living from higher values, self-indulgence will take over, and everything will be difficult. You may still gain the blessings life has to give; however, they could be lost in the end. So pay attention to what you've been given. The expression of gratitude will create the strongest foundation for love and longevity.

If you are considering this relationship, know that it's a blessed connection when both parties appreciate what they are being given and share their good fortune with others. Take the high road and enjoy the amazing gifts it has to offer! Let your intuition be your guide.

The Keys to the Kingdom of the Ten of Diamonds

Choose the High Road

You and your partner must always choose the highest road of integrity for the greatest results and rewards. The Ten of Diamonds is a very powerful card. The high side of this influence represents the values of humanity, and it is ruled by integrity. When you are forthright in your living of life, you get the blessings. When you aren't, you get the challenges. The secret to right action will be found in listening to and following your intuition at all times.

Sharing Your Blessings

Because this card bestows life with good fortune, as its ambassadors, you'll have the opportunity to give to others who are less fortunate. Of course, you must give to one another as well. The unconscious side of this card can be very selfish, so avoid self-indulgent behaviors. An added challenge with this card is its misperception that it's never getting enough—of anything. Its desires are insatiable. For this reason, the conscious expression of gratitude is even more important. Gratitude births generosity, which inspires you to give in ways that make a difference.

Conviction

If you work hard for what you want, you will always get it, albeit sometimes in the final hour. When you think that you've worked hard enough, there may be a greater force involved, one that knows where you're holding back. The Ten of Diamonds influence aims to bring out the best in us, because nothing less will do. You must remember at all times that your efforts are expressions of gratitude for the blessings that you have and will receive. Your effort must be motivated by conviction. Be grateful first, work hard second, and give thanks in the end.

Conscious Listening

Conscious listening is a must! You must listen to your intuition, and you must listen to your partner. And in both cases, you have to listen with total presence of being. This is absolutely necessary for the survival of the relationship. The energy in this connection can create a monumental focus on self, which can be great, as long as you realize that you're not the only one in the relationship.

37
Jack of Diamonds
An Unconventional Journey

This composite can create a very tricky relationship environment, as there can be an element of fantasy and illusion shrouding the mind of the Jack of Diamonds, especially when it comes to love and romance. The planet Neptune, who is the ruler of fantasy and illusion, is the ruling planet of this card. Care must be taken to keep things realistic, clear, and exact. This jack is also strongly influenced by the planet Uranus, which is unpredictable, eclectic, and sometimes erratic. Together, these two planetary influences can create a somewhat unconventional, and quite often peculiar, type of relationship. Tradition will not work with this connection at all. So if you're seeking something unusual and eclectic, you may have found what you were looking for. If you are more interested in having a traditional relationship, you might want to think twice.

Responsibility is a key word for the Jack of Diamonds. As with all jacks, there is a bounty of cleverness to draw from, and it can be all too easy to be irresponsible or cunning. This self-serving energy can actually show up in the relationship, and you should take care not to give in to it. On the other hand, this same energy is highly creative when applied to business, and this can be an excellent connection for working as business partners. This relationship has the potential to evoke unlimited creativity that can be applied in any way imaginable, and you're likely to find that you also become more inspired to explore new avenues of creativity.

Working together is an excellent way to balance the unique energies found in this connection. Integrate your dreams with practical applications of productivity, individually and as a couple, and you will create great success and even receive recognition for it. Balance your distinctive ideas with concrete actions to produce material gain, as doing so will enhance and stabilize your relationship.

There can be a tendency to wear rose-colored glasses in this relationship. It's crucial to know when to remove them so that you can see clearly to make important decisions. Logic and reason will be your best friends when those times arise, and you must consult them for practical matters.

Family and marriage can play a strong role in this relationship, and you may find yourself giving energy to both throughout your time together. Strong bonds with family and friends create a solid foundation of support.

There's a characteristic within this card that chooses to be secretive and at times isolated. You might find yourselves adopting these tendencies, and if you do, they should be honored. Share with others only the things that you know they are going to support. Everything else you must keep between the two of you and hold as sacred.

This connection has a bit of a wacky energy weaving through it. You'll have to allow yourselves to be true individuals if you really are to reap this card's greatest benefits. Confinement equals frustration for this jack. Be open and eclectic, and have fun! One thing is for sure: you have the power to create anything in this relationship. So why not create the relationship you want? Just be sure it fits with the unique qualities of this card's personality. If you can appreciate the gift of creative inspiration that comes with this connection, you'll have a great time together. Let go of your expectations of how you think the relationship should be, and embrace whatever it is that is happening between the two of you.

If you're presently in this relationship, heed the practical applications suggested in order to bring balance and stability into your partnership. Balancing reality and fantasy will be essential to the lasting success of this connection. If something's bothering you right now, apply the wisdom of the cards to give things a boost and put your relationship back on track.

If you are considering or exploring this connection as a possibility for yourself, please know that you might be looking through those rose-colored glasses mentioned earlier. You need to fully explore what benefits will be brought into your life by entering this relationship. If you don't see any, it might be wise to think twice. The bottom line here is listening to your belly and doing what feels right. If you enjoy your freedom and seek to be in a non-traditional relationship, you have struck gold!

The Keys to the Kingdom of the Jack of Diamonds

Creative Authenticity

Authentic personal expression—through your work, your hobbies, and your personal interests—is your number one priority in this relationship. If you choose to do something together, support one another's full self-expression. The Jack of Diamonds is a highly creative influence, especially when it comes to making money. If the motivation is there, go for it! Music is very much inspired and appreciated by this jack, as is history. This is an excellent influence for facilitating consulting, counseling, and anything artistic.

Home and Family

Home and family will be the foundation of this relationship's strength and longevity. Create the perfect space, if you live together, to house your interests and support your need for comfort. Being with friends and family and sharing your dreams are essential, and time must be allotted for these things.

Explore the Unusual

Embrace the eclectic nature of this very unusual connection by allowing yourself to be completely free in your creative expression. You must think outside the box, do what makes yourself happy, and explore the reasonable unknown with your partner. Most importantly, enjoy discovering each other on a daily basis.

Freedom

Freedom is the first, middle, and last name of the Jack of Diamonds. The freedom to be, to express, and to explore is necessary for both of you. Remember to give one another the space and trust to do your own thing. This gift of individual freedom will provide a refreshing quality that enables you to grow as a couple.

38

Queen of Diamonds

Structures of Entitlement

The Queen of Diamonds is a highly creative, amazingly intelligent card. This, however, is not the easiest life path for a relationship in the deck, and the challenges are most often felt in the areas of relating and/or finances. If these struggles persist, they will be reflected in the relationship. When the creative intelligence of this card is applied with discipline in a direction that is supported by higher values, great things can be accomplished. When this is not the choice, frustration in communication and worry about money will override the goodness of this connection.

With this diamond queen comes a love for the finer things in life. Her royal tastes and desire to live in a grand way often mean that you will have to work hard to support your passions. You may also want to use your innate gifts to give back to life in some way. It will be necessary to reassess your values on a regular basis to keep yourselves on track and to keep the relationship growing in healthy ways. This queen struggles with issues of entitlement. There can be a subconscious battle between feeling entitled and feeling undeserving. This unconscious battle might make an appearance from time to time in your relationship; if it does, the secret to winning the battle will be found in loving yourself.

Outward expressions of love will be the secret to making this relationship work. If you run into disappointment, it's because your expectations are taking you for a ride. This queen is famous for having unreasonable expectations. Dissatisfaction with yourself or your partner is a sign that you need to lower your expectations, remember what you love about yourself or your partner, and assume a position of gratefulness. Selflessness can be a challenge with this connection and must be observed. Shower your partner with gifts. These should be things that you know he or she wants. This queen loves toys—toys for the men, finery for the ladies. And both the king and the queen of the diamond suit love surprises. Having fun together and sharing the things that each of you cherish is essential for making this relationship a happy experience for both of you.

This connection can stir up worry regarding money and security, and these things need to be talked about and kept in perspective. On the other side of this worry is the gift of financial creativity. If money worries come up, ask yourself how you can be more creative with your finances. Find new ways to think about and be with your money. Worry itself can be alleviated through physical activities or creative artistic expression. The feelings of uncertainty that can arise in this relationship need to be addressed, or they will burrow into the foundation of your togetherness and destroy it.

If you're in this relationship, please take the time to be present with and receptive to your partner. Drama can reign in this connection, and it often comes from one of you not feeling heard by the other. The underbelly of this card is one that houses real insecurities, and they may be felt at times. To offset uncertainty, be affectionate and reinforce your love verbally by saying, "I love you." Make time to play together, as this will nurture the innocence that is hidden in this card. Be open, honest, and direct with your communication, and avoid unnecessary drama. No projection allowed! The trick is to treat your partner as you would like to be treated without expecting the same in return.

If you're considering a Queen of Diamonds partnership, know that it is not the easiest relationship path. It demands self-discipline, right thought, and right action. Without these, things can become frustrating, to say the least. You're putting yourself in a situation where you will be constantly learning about values, giving, patience, and pride. However, it's quite possible that some part of you wants these lessons, and this is why you've drawn this relationship to you.

The Keys to the Kingdom of the Queen of Diamonds

Acceptance

Acceptance is key. It's all too easy to place unreasonable expectations on your partner—and on yourself, for that matter. Lower your expectations and see your partner for who he or she really is rather than who you expect him or her to be. See what you love, and feel and express your gratitude. Understanding the importance of gratitude in this relationship is very important.

Outward Expressions of Love

Outward displays of love and affection are crucial. Express your love physically, verbally, and consistently. The underlying insecurity that accompanies this card suggests that the more demonstrative you are in your expressions of love and gratitude, the more stability there will be in yourselves and the relationship.

Tell the Truth

Tell your partner what is true for you. Honesty is imperative. Share with one another. If your partner is gone and you miss him or her, say so. Speak, speak, and speak about what's going on inside you. However, if you are upset about something, make sure that you get straight in your own mind what's really going on before speaking to your partner about it. Do not bring the past into this relationship! It will surely kill it. Be in the present, and build something special together that belongs only to the two of you.

Innocence and Self-Love

First and foremost, you must cultivate your love for yourself. You are only able to love another as much as you love yourself. Know that you deserve what you have been given. Embrace confidence rather than false pride. See your own beauty in the eyes of your partner. Then, with the curiosity and innocence of a child, explore yourself, each other, and the world around you. New learning, new toys, new places, new people, and new music—all are important. Whatever your interests are, be sure to stay active with them.

39
King *of* Diamonds
Choosing the Crown

T he King of Diamonds is often referred to as the card of the successful businessman. This king actually governs higher values, the art of manifestation, and right action. This relationship must have a strong spiritual base to operate from, or it will not work. The power inherent in this card is tremendous, and it can lead to stubborn behaviors and power struggles if the ego, mind, and emotions are not kept in check with self-awareness.

Given that this king rules the realms of values and finance, both of these arenas will be major focal points in the relationship—for good, ill, or otherwise. If the higher principles of integrity are not understood properly, this relationship will prove to be very challenging for both of you. Some of the lessons that accompany this connection have to do with maintaining integrity toward money and values; if you have any issues with either of these things, they will be challenged. This can be a very good working relationship if you have common goals and ambitions.

You are drawn to or are in this relationship to learn to acknowledge, embrace, and express your personal power. Much good can come out of this relationship when you take responsibility for the goodness of being and for life itself. The King of Diamonds is a very generous, loving connection. This king is also filled with passion. The power of this card is tremendous, and you can literally manifest anything you want once you align with the higher aspects of this card, which come from the true laws of abundance. It is this king's good fortune to create abundance for others. In doing so, everything is given. Selfishness is not an option.

Friends and associates are likely to be people of means, position, and intelligence, as this king draws such people as a reflection of his crown. Fine living and beautiful surroundings will be important as well. Travel, outdoor activities, and physical exercise are extremely important for keeping things healthy and happy, as there is a constant influx of mental energy that must be kept in balance. Creative expression is essential, and together you will come up with many great ideas. Take action with those ideas, and they are likely to lead you to success.

The strong material desires that are spawned by this relationship must be balanced with love, and in doing so, you will find happiness. This card can foster tendencies toward one-sided behaviors, so you must cultivate open, receptive attitudes; pay attention and really listen. The nature of the king is to rule, and the qualities of leadership will be brought forth in each of your personalities.

One of the most important things you have to watch out for with this influence is the fact that this king is not too adept at expressing feelings, as he assumes that the other party already knows what his feelings are. You must remember to express to your partner what you're feeling and thinking. Don't assume that he or she knows what's going on. Communicate.

If you are presently in this relationship, know that love, adventure, play, spending time outdoors, and being open and receptive to one another's ideas will keep it positive and growing. Make the expression of thoughts and feelings standard conduct; express your love through your affection, actions, and words.

If you are considering this relationship, be sure that you're up for the challenge of having your *will* tested on a regular basis. Be honest with yourself and only enter this relationship if you know 100 percent, with all of your heart, that it is right for you. It's likely that you've drawn this relationship to yourself to learn to stand in your own personal power and to have love, compassion, and understanding for yourself and others. This can be a great relationship—one that is filled with love, passion, adventure, and great experiences of creating your reality together.

The Keys to the Kingdom of the King of Diamonds

Be Open and Receptive

The keys that unlock the doors of the King of Diamonds relationship are receptivity and openness in communication. This connection can evoke power struggles. Being open to your partner and his or her ideas, thoughts, and expressions can really help to tame the ego that wants to rear its head.

Displays of Affection

Verbal and physical expressions of passion are more than important for the health and growth of this relationship and for each of you to feel comfortable, safe, and secure. There's an element of assumption with this card that can cause the two of you to forget to be openly expressive with your emotions and your affections. The King of Diamonds is a very loving influence. However, it can miss what's really going on in a relationship and easily overlook the important gestures that make things feel yummy. Remember to express what you're thinking and feeling about your partner.

Support Your Creativity

This is a highly creative influence, and it's likely that the two of you are going to come up with a lot of great ideas. Remember, this king likes to do business, make money, and wheel and deal. These influences could easily stimulate more ideas than you know what to do with. The secret is to focus on the ones that light your fires of passion and take them to fruition. Action is the key!

Intentional Communication

Thoughtful communication is a major key to your success. For this king, the law requires verbal connecting one-on-one. There can be no exceptions. Without intentional communication, uncertainty and confusion will take form and escort your minds into feelings of insecurity and then to separation. All of this can be avoided with conversation. If your partner is interested in something, acknowledge his or her interest and the value it has for him or her. Be genuine in your interest and your support.

40
Ace of Spades
The Path of Transformation

This powerful card, known as the magi or magician, is the keeper of secrets, mysteries, and ancient wisdoms. The king of all the aces, the Ace of Spades is an initiator of personal and professional transformation. In a relationship, this card unites passion with intent, creating a fast-moving, determined energy that, when directed, can be unstoppable. There's an element of singularity personified in this card that will be present in your connection with one another. For this reason, it's suggested that you and your partner have shared spiritual experiences or practices at the foundation of your relationship.

Deep personal transformation is guaranteed to occur for both of you, which is why like-minded thinking and common spiritual values are essential. Without these foundational elements, this relationship will be confronted with recurring obstacles. These obstacles will mostly take place in your communication and will be the result of each of you not hearing what your partner is saying. The secret to transforming communication from challenging to productive is to actively listen to one another with genuine interest. To be present to listen, you will have to capture the intense, outwardly focused energy of this ace and direct it inward to still your minds. Conscious listening can be one of the greatest challenges hidden in the Ace of Spades relationship. Learn to listen with 100 percent of your attention. Listening, although it is the greatest challenge for this card, is the key to success in this relationship. You'll have to listen like you have never listened before. And you must listen with your heart and your whole being. Conscious effort here will be necessary, because learning to listen is one of this card's lifelong lessons.

There can be a challenging dynamic between the desire for spiritual advancement and the desire for material gain. The truth is, both are possible at the same time. Pursuing both will certainly ensure the success and good fortune of your relationship and support your individual attainment of wisdom.

Emotional and material fears may surface, demanding your attention. Ultimately, the transformation that occurs from dealing with the fear brings about positive change. Your best choice in these times will be to embrace the change with appreciation for what it brings. Gratitude is always the key. Be grateful for what you have by focusing on that rather than the challenges. The challenges embody opportunities; you must embrace the challenge in order for the opportunity to reveal itself to you. Without gratitude, you will feel as though you are swimming up a huge waterfall, constantly making effort and getting nowhere.

The truth is, it can take a lot of effort to be in this relationship. It can be challenging. That's why it's so important to have a strong spiritual connection and shared values. Having these things will support you in meeting these challenges with gusto. It will also enable you to gain the many rewards this ace has to offer—rewards in the realms of personal development and material achievement. However, if you don't pay attention to your shared spirituality or values, or if you lack these important things, conflict and misunderstanding can become an all-too-familiar and most destructive pattern.

Openness in your communication with one another is an absolute must! You cannot withhold anything in the partnership, as doing so will create unbearable emotional pain and damage the heart and soul of your relationship. You must dream together, inspire one another, and create together. You will be required to protect the privacy of your relationship from the world around you, as others may try to interfere in it. Outside interference will result in the rapid decline of joy and pleasure. Champion your connection always. When issues come up, don't talk with your friends—talk with each other.

If you are currently in this relationship and running into challenges, take to heart what is being said and use the information to turn things around, if that is what your heart desires. This relationship will shine its brightest when both of you are on the same page with your own individual paths in life. That doesn't mean that you have to express yourselves in related ways in the world; however, you do need to have similar intentions when it comes to self-cultivation and your values in life. There's real magic to be found in this union. It may not always be easy to find, but it's there in spades, waiting to be discovered in each and every moment. Be light and receptive rather than weighing yourself down with being overly serious about things. This connection challenges the ego. Learn to be more impersonal. Be encouraging and supportive rather than critical and judgmental. Look for the magic, and let it guide you to new ways of being—both with yourself and in your relationship.

If you have attracted this relationship to yourself, it's likely that deep inside you exists a tremendous desire to go beyond a physical union and submerge yourself into trust and intimacy. This experience may be a challenge initially; however, achieving this depth of trust is the very opportunity that comes with this connection. Trust what you feel and know it to be true within you. The personal transformation that can take place in this relationship is awesome. If you see the value in that and you embrace this partnership with clear intent, the growth you experience will bring about profound changes that will serve you for the rest of your life. However, if you're not interested in this type of committed personal growth and self-cultivation, this relationship may not be right for you. You're the only one who really knows.

The Keys to the Kingdom of the Ace of Spades

Be Grateful

You must make gratitude a real, heartfelt experience. Make the choice to be grateful for what you have. Conscious intention in this way will turn challenges into the golden opportunities that they really are. Express your gratitude; make it tangible. The more you express love and appreciation, the greater your rewards will be, both personally and in your relationship as a whole.

Shared Intention

Values must be shared—and the higher they are, the better. You and your partner must be aligned with your intentions regarding the things that are most important in life. Share with one another, and do things together to support your beliefs. Cultivate your spiritual lives, your characters, and your earthly treasures, together. What your values are is not as important as the fact that they match. By not cultivating those things that are most important, you risk weakening the foundation of your relationship—or destroying it altogether.

Trust

Learning to trust in a way that you have not done before could be a large part of why you have drawn this relationship to you. The cultivation of this trust will come through your sharing. Openness in your communication is the key that unlocks the door to trust. Trust yourself and trust your partner, and express your trust through your communication and behavior. Choose to be open and receptive to what your partner has to say or wants to share. Embrace and take to heart what is important to her, and express your interest through actions that he can hear, feel, and see. Secrets are not allowed in this kingdom.

Privacy

As a couple, you must guard your privacy very carefully. Others may want to interfere or give you advice. Forget it! Don't go to others for advice. Don't talk to your friends and family about your personal concerns or even about what you're doing. Talk to one another. If necessary, seek professional help if challenges arise. But do not seek help from friends or family, as this can create serious unwanted experiences that you will regret. Be mature in your way of being together, and honor your connection.

41

Two of Spades

Love and Wisdom in Friendship

Here we have the hand of destiny at work. There is no question that this meeting was meant to happen, and this fated union is charged with power and wisdom for each of you to draw from. Because this is a two relationship, cooperation, communication, nurturing, and romance are the assets that create the strongest foundation for love and longevity. Giving and receiving and love and kindness open the doors to unlimited possibilities for self-expression and personal power, for each of you as individuals and for both of you as a couple. You must take care to temper the power that is inherent in this composite, and it must be moderated through acts of giving and through the cultivation of your friendship.

Together you will dream in very big ways. It will be important to embrace your dreaming, as it's in the sharing of your dreams and your visions that you each rise to new heights in your personal awareness and the articulation of your selves. This relationship asks you to have the courage to think outside the box. As your true essences emerge, together you will grow and become full with your self-expression. It's likely that you called this relationship to yourself in order to dive more deeply into your innate wisdom and self-knowledge, and to learn how to express your wisdom in the world around you. The wisdom of this spade will ask you to be practical with your choices and decisions as you travel in your journey of togetherness.

The planet Neptune rules this card, so living near the water or visiting it frequently will be important for both of you. Neptune governs the imagination, so as you travel through new emotional states of mind, you must maintain balance between that which is real and that which is fantasy. Learn to flow, like the water, keeping things moving in a forward direction with your emotional maturity. This can be a dreamy connection, and one that deserves time for intimate exploration. On the other side, there can be a tendency toward becoming overly analytical. A harmonious balance must be found between the two. Giving way and being receptive are ways to overcome the fixed attitudes that can be an influence of the spade suit. Cultivating your friendship will enhance this relationship more than anything. Emotional fulfillment results when dreams and reality are balanced through the sharing of kindness and wisdom.

Routines and repetitious patterns will stifle the energy of your relationship. It's important to not only keep these downturns from happening, but also to initiate activities and interests to keep things moving forward. Both endeavors will keep this relationship alive and thriving. Together you must learn, share, and teach. The Two of Spades is a teacher of wisdom. The card actually symbolizes the sharing of wisdom. Being in the relationship, you will gather knowledge, integrate it into your understanding, and share it with others.

If you are presently in this relationship and experiencing challenges—which can manifest as arguments, headstrong behavior, and isolation—stop and remember why you were drawn to your partner initially. What was the attraction? That is the very thing that you need to hang onto, remember, and look for in times when you choose to pull away. Apply the secrets that make this relationship the best it can be. A two relationship has tremendous potential for longevity, as long as each of you looks to your partner to see yourself and chooses the higher expressions of the two: cooperation, consideration, and communication. Codependency, conflict, and confrontation lead directly to disaster.

It's likely that you've known one another in a past life. To make right choices in the present one regarding the direction you wish to take, you must first look at what is going on inside you. Each of you must take 100-percent responsibility for looking inside yourself as an individual. Remember that expressions of love and kindness will always take this relationship out of stress and into romance. Romance is a major key for its success and happiness. You're in this relationship to learn how to communicate with wisdom and compassion.

Give all you can, and use the wisdom of the cards to change your relationship. If you don't find happiness in doing that, then perhaps it's time to move on. Make the Keys to the Kingdom of this relationship your priorities, and you can build a strong and lasting relationship together. When things are off, or you're feeling like you're not getting what you need, it's time to nurture yourself and then your partner. It's also a sign that you must take your communication to a deeper, more intimate level. Doing so will reestablish harmony, cooperation, greater understanding, and compassion.

If you are drawn to this relationship, know that in it you will learn to choose whether or not to be more mature and expressive of who and how you are in partnership. This can be a great connection that brings wonderful blessings. However, you must be ready to give of yourself, and let go of any and all old ways of being that do not serve you or a relationship.

The Keys to the Kingdom of the Two of Spades

Communication and Cooperation

How the two of you cooperate together and communicate with one another will either make or break this relationship. A lack of commitment in these areas will create conflict and lead to chaos and disorder in the forms of arguments and stubborn behaviors. Drop your guard and be open, receptive, and supportive of your partner. Remember, this person is your friend. Wisdom is a doorway into the unknown and all that is possible, and it will be developed through your verbal interaction, exploration of self and each other, and the discoveries you make in those journeys. Choose to be wise, mature, and authentic in all of your exchanges.

Dreaming Your Reality

The nature of this connection is dreamy, and your imaginations are gateways into the future of your lives together. Nurture one another and your dreams. Feed each other's intellect by sharing new learning, things of importance, and your dreams and fantasies. Openly displaying affection and respect for one another will build trust. Dream together and apart, and share your dreams in creative ways.

Romance

Romance is key to keeping things alive and juicy. Think ahead and be creative with how you express your love. Make time for romantic adventures, even if they are at home. Candlelight dinners, sunset walks, slow dancing, picnics, or date nights together—all of these types of experiences will keep your relationship healthy and insure its longevity.

Share Your Wisdom

The Two of Spades represents the sharing of wisdom. As you and your partner grow as a couple and incorporate the wisdom you gather from your learning experiences as individuals and as a couple, you will find opportunities to share with others in meaningful ways. This is vital for your relationship. You are meant to be teachers of others in some way, whether they be children or adults. Be on the watch for opportunities that provide a platform for you to step into the roles of teaching, sharing, or counseling.

42

Three of Spades

The Mysterious Journey

The Three of Spades unites the elements of spirituality and practicality. Self-discipline and the application of wisdom are strong traits of this card. Many important lessons can be learned in this relationship. One of the major learning opportunities will involve honoring and trusting your intuition more, as this relationship may not always be what it appears to be.

There is an element of the invisible with this connection. You must acknowledge and pay attention to gut feelings and subtle intuitions, as doing so will develop and enhance your perceptual skills. I am not suggesting that there will be deceit in this relationship. The Three of Spades embodies an element of the mysterious, and it likes privacy. The combination of those two elements can leave you feeling as though your partner is not always 100-percent available or visible. These feelings can create an underlying sense of uncertainty. Trust in your perception, and your partner will help keep your relationship together. Without trust, suspicion may arise at times. Understand that great inner strength and confidence will be needed to feel secure with this connection.

Perhaps you were attracted to this person because you want to learn to have more balance in your life. This card says, "Observe, think, then act." You may feel as if this person is a wish fulfilled or a dream come true. It's also possible that your first encounter revolved around some sort of physical activity or spiritual event. Physical activity will help you to maintain mental and emotional balance and must be a constant for the two of you. The same must be true of spirituality if you are to establish a common ground of comfort and stability. Meaningful conversations and physical activities will be essential. Without these, there can be uncertainty and confusion, self-doubt, and feelings of insecurity for both of you.

Chitchat is not conversation in this relationship, and in excess it can lead to boredom. Both of you will have to guard against speaking with a forked tongue, which is a danger with this connection, even if it's not your nature. Anger and drama will be signs that things are too superficial and that communication needs to go deeper. Honesty must be the foundation of your communication, for if it's not, the very core of your relationship will be poisoned.

Being drawn to or attracting a Three of Spades relationship reflects a need to release old negative thought patterns that surround or inhibit the success of partnership. These old patterns were most likely developed during childhood. For this reason, it's important to reject anything that resembles abuse or disrespect. The Three of Spades is a highly sophisticated intelligence, and you must respect your partner's innate wisdom. That respect must be shown in the form of honesty and truthfulness.

The energetic composition of this partnership is blessed with a creative intelligence that must be expressed. Incorporate a variety of entertaining ventures to keep interest alive and your connection moving forward. Traditional ways of being together must be spiced up with new experiences. Having fun together can take the edge off of the intense emotional learning that takes place with this composite. This can be a challenging relationship for many. Trust, listen to, and act upon what you really feel. For some, this can be a great relationship; for many, it can be challenging.

If you are presently in this relationship and feel uncertain, it may be helpful for you to know uncertainty is a common feeling for this connection. The Three of Spades is a highly creative card—quite brilliant, actually—and those creative juices must have pathways to flow through, otherwise insecurity begins to brew. You can't be codependent in this relationship. You have to be strong, independent, and focused on the expression of your individual creativity, whether that expression be through your work or your personal endeavors. It's important to balance your feelings with rational thinking when things seem uncertain. If you feel disconnected, rip away the veil of separation between you and your partner and proceed with open eyes.

If you are considering this relationship, the most important thing you can do for yourself is notice how you feel when you are with this person. If you feel secure, confident, happy, and free to be yourself when you are together, then explore it further. If you have reservations or underlying feelings of uncertainty, take more time and do not commit until you feel certain.

The Keys to the Kingdom of the Three of Spades

Truthfulness
Truthfulness is essential. Anything else will lead straight to mistrust and suspicion, which will rot the foundation of your relationship. No white lies, no little fibs, not even with your thoughts, are allowed if this connection is to be solid.

Authenticity
Genuine behavior and expression of feelings will create feelings of safety at the emotional-physical level for both of you. It's important for the feelings of security to be physically felt as well as known emotionally. Actions and words must align.

Self-Expression
Self-expression will be important for each of you, and you will have to give one another the freedom to be the individuals that you are.

There's an offbeat element to this connection, and you must allow space for the unusual.

Resolution of the Past

Resolution of the past may be a running theme throughout this relationship. You should uncover and pay attention to the details of your past on your own, and then decide whether or not to share your personal learning with your partner. Do your own work first, and then let it go. Bring fresh new energy into this relationship, and it will thrive.

43

Four *of* Spades

Determination

The appreciation of art, beauty, language, and intelligence is high on the list of priorities with this relationship connection, and it will be brought forth in each of you. The sharing of these things will cultivate your experience of being together. In fact, it may be that you first met at a social event having to do with one of the above.

This relationship has the potential to bring forth your artistic nature, and the effects could very well show up in your physical environment. It will be essential for you to be surrounded by beauty so that your senses are satisfied in every way by your immediate environment. The intense appreciation for beauty and comfort that accompanies this card can lead to overindulgence or overspending, so you might have to balance fiscal responsibility and your desire for beautiful things. Also, there can be a danger of creating such a perfect space of comfort that you'll forget the world and become like hermits. Therefore, socializing is imperative to keep the energy of this partnership moving. You must propagate your social life by getting out and about on a regular basis.

This is a fortune relationship connection, so embrace it with gratitude, as appreciation will make it grow strong and last long. The foundation of this relationship has very much to do with creating stability and security in all aspects of life. This connection is about building solid foundations in your inner and outer worlds.

Home, family, and friends will be positioned at the top of your priority list.

The challenges that can show up with this connection have to do with personal willfulness and the need to be in control. The Four of Spades is an extremely fixed energy. Often one of you will get stuck in how you are thinking and, in doing so, expect your partner to agree with you. In life, things are not black and white; however, to the Four of Spades they are—even if they are actually purple and green. This energy will emerge between you in the relationship, and you will bear witness to your strongest will. When this willfulness shows its face, the wisest choice you can make is to acknowledge your stubbornness and yield in the situation. Learning to yield is part of the teaching this card has to offer.

You must take care and time in your communication so that you keep it clear and open. Receptivity, openness, and listening are the challenges and opportunities of this relationship. You must make use of your very best listening skills and listen with a truly open heart and mind. If you think you're being receptive, but you're still opposing what your partner is saying, you are not actually being receptive. This is really important to understand. The Four of Spades can be deaf and blind to the thoughts and feelings of others. If these communication issues arise in your relationship, the question you have to ask yourself is, "Do I want to be right or do I want to be loved?" It should be an easy choice, but, honestly, I think the Four of Spades would rather be right. You may already find it easy to be open and committed to listening; however, if you don't, issues regarding these abilities will show up as your teachers.

Engaging in activities of all kinds together will be important for the health of this relationship. It can be all too easy to get lost in doing your own thing and forget that the relationship itself is like a flower that needs to be watered and nourished continuously. Grow this relationship with good communication, openness and receptivity, lovingkindness, and lots of play, and you will have a happy, healthy, long-lasting experience of love. If you don't give it your proper attention and participation, it will be a difficult struggle to the end.

If you are presently in this relationship and dealing with willful battles, perhaps step back and be more open and receptive. If you feel that you're not being heard, listen more. If you feel that your partner's not open, be more open yourself. Remember, the person that stands before you is a mirror of you. This partnership naturally challenges you to think in new ways, and it's wise to take the initiative in learning these new ways for the growth of yourself and your relationship. Otherwise, communication will be a struggle, and the overly serious nature of this card will put out the fires of passion.

If you're exploring the possibility of having this relationship, know that your personal will is going to be more forceful, which might be one reason you are attracted to this person. If you create a solid foundation, this relationship has the power to be long lasting. Building the foundations must be a conscious choice and sincere effort.

The Keys to the Kingdom of the Four of Spades

Openness and Receptivity

You might find at times that you have to make extra effort to be open and receptive to your partner, especially if paying attention is not your forte. You can show your openness and receptivity simply by being present. Monitor your thinking and filter it through your feeling self before it comes out of your mouth or through your actions. It's all too easy to adopt routine behaviors with this relationship, so it's important to be like a child with your receptivity and meet each day with a fresh new attitude of love.

Active Listening

Listening can be the biggest challenge for the Four of Spades. Within the character of this card is a strong, innate sense of responsibility, which will manifest through communication. It's essential that you be attentive with your listening and that you learn to listen with your feelings. Avoid getting into confrontational battles of the will.

Be Active and Socialize

Social activities are crucial for the health and well-being of this relationship. Take time and make plans to do things together, especially activities having to do with travel, art, and music. The intelligence of this card needs to be fed with that which is rich and meaningful, otherwise it becomes stuck in routines and stagnates. Also be sure to make time to be social with friends, family, and groups of people who share your interests.

Intimacy

It's important to create time for intimacy. Passion must be expressed, shared, explored, and discovered. Create special times and special places to foster the expression of the juicy side of this card. Bring romance into the relationship in natural, beautiful ways.

44

Five of Spades

The Wild Ride of Change

The Five of Spades is the most powerful representative of change. When you have this card as a relationship composite, things can seem to move faster than the speed of light and in multiple directions all at once. If you're not grounded and centered within yourself and with your personal direction in life, this energy can throw you off balance or turn your life upside down. Changes in your lifestyle are almost guaranteed with this relationship connection, and at the very least, diversity will show up on a constant basis. You will feel right at home here if this number is a strong influence for you personally.

You and your partner are likely to become popular as a result of this card influence, and you can anticipate being in great demand with friends and family. Travel and variety are musts, as this partnership must have elements of adventure, change, and variety to thrive. With the abundance of creative juice that comes with this card, you might find that you express yourself in new ways. It's important to understand that the fast-moving energy of the Five of Spades can sometimes make it difficult to stabilize ambitions, goals, or plans long enough to bring them to fruition. Like all fives, this card thrives on experience rather than accomplishment. If you're used to having things solid, stable, and structured, this relationship will change that dynamic for sure and could bring about feelings of frustration or uncertainty. If you prefer consistency and sameness, you will have an opportunity to become more at ease with change in this relationship.

Desire and attraction stand in the spotlight with this connection, and these are likely to have been part of your initial experience upon meeting for the first time—and the second, and the third. You might find that you express your emotions with more dramatic flare or that they swing a bit more than usual. Emotional mastery is called for, and achieving it is your opportunity here. Without mental-emotional balance, things have the potential to get pretty wild. The secret to keeping balance within you and between the two of you lies in your ability to communicate with your own mind and with your partner. Clear thinking is needed in this relationship to keep things in their proper perspective. There is a lot of movement with this connection. Everything that can change is likely to, especially relative to careers. Changes will be for the better in the long run.

Demonstrations of respect are imperative. You must have variety in your life together; play together, explore the day and night together, go on adventures, take walks, go out and gaze at the stars together, and create together. Play, play, and then play some more. All of this is necessary to keep this relationship balanced and healthy. Socialize and get out and party with your friends, make new acquaintances, step outside normal routines, and this relationship will be a happy one. Fall into a rut with routines, schedules, and idle time, and this connection will be a time bomb with a short fuse waiting to blow.

If you're in this relationship presently and finding aspects of it to be challenging, cultivate your understanding of your self and your partner in a new and deeper way. Take to heart the information that is in this report and apply it. This connection can be a tough experience for those who like everything to be and stay in order. If you have a five or three birth card yourself, then you might feel right at home here. If you are a two, four, eight, or any other of the even numbers, it might be a bit challenging; however, it can also be great fun.

If you're considering this relationship, pay attention. If you start dating this person and your life starts turning upside down, step back and see if that's what you want, because change will only continue to occur. The upside is that your creative intelligence will be well fed by this connection, and the Five of Spades has the potential to take you on a major journey of self-discovery and self-expression. All you have to do to take this ride is leave your past behind.

The Keys to the Kingdom of the Five of Spades

Creativity

This is one of the most creative cards in the deck, and it's sure to spur you and your partner in new directions with your creativity, one way or another. Give way to the new ideas and new way of thinking that are initiated in this relationship. Take action with the ideas that come to you. You might find that follow-through is not your strongest point with this card ruling the kingdom; however, if you give yourself permission to "do it all," you will thrive. Remember, this path is about experience, and eventually, you will do what you set out to do. You just might not do it in a straight line or a linear way. That's okay. Enjoy the diversity and make the fast-moving, eclectic energy of this card your friend and source of inspiration.

Diversity

Play, adventure, work, exploration, and anything new, different, and unfamiliar—all are favored with this connection. Not only are they favored, but they're also absolutely necessary. You cannot possibly get into any kind of rut here, or you will be tying yourselves and the relationship into knots. Initiate adventure and variety into this relationship so that they don't come looking for you unexpectedly. When they do, the topsy-turvy stuff happens. If you don't feed the relationship with diversity, it goes looking for its own food.

Emotional Mastery

Emotional mastery is called for, and developing it will be your opportunity. You will have opportunities to heal the past and to let go of old beliefs, wounds, and fears having to do with love, intimacy, and relationship. Give yourself permission to explore new ways of being in relationship and new ways of sharing yourself. Choose to be on a path of self-cultivation, and learn to reap the greatest rewards in this partnership. Most importantly, be diligent with your efforts, honest with yourself, and present with your partner.

Mutual Support

This connection demands that you give and receive support. You will each have, and perhaps also have together, projects or interests that you want to pursue. It's crucial that you support one another totally and do whatever you can to enhance each other's experiences. The rewards you experience when you do will be unlimited and all inspiring. You will have only to gain in the greatest ways.

45

Six *of* Spades

The Fantasy of Love

You must have felt the hands of fate and destiny working in your life when this meeting occurred. This is a very dreamy connection, and if you're not careful, you could just drift away into a fantasy—and then into another and another. This is the card of the dreamer. It's also a card that says this meeting was meant to be. Where it goes is a choice, of course, and you can be quite certain that you two have known one another before, either in this lifetime or another. This is an inspired, intelligent, artistic card, which can be prone to escapism, irresponsibility, and dreaminess, so you must take charge to keep things moving in the direction of reality. Practice and diligence will be needed to see things as they really are rather than getting lost in fantasy and illusion—for good or bad. You will love being in love, and you will thrive on the romance and beauty of it all. Ultimately, this can be an awesome connection; it's simply a matter of being clear, honest, and realistic with yourself and your partner.

Your relationship will be unique and at the same time a bit unusual. Making adjustments and compromises will be givens; you will always be re-creating your partnership in creative ways, while reinventing yourselves as individuals at the same time. Kindness and curiosity go hand-in-hand here, so be sure to avoid getting caught in fixed attitudes. Sixes are the keepers of balance and harmony, graciousness and receptivity; however, they can also be very argumentative and stubborn, and that energy is likely to manifest in some way or another from time to time. Observing your behaviors and learning to resonate with your own natural rhythms, while understanding those of your partner, will serve you well and keep things harmonious. Home and physical surroundings will have the utmost importance, and it will be vital for you to surround yourselves with harmony and beauty. For the Six of Spades, a living space is a sanctuary of beauty, peace, and love.

Individually, there will be a need for independence and autonomy. This means that you must respect one another as individuals and support each other in your efforts to manifest who you are in the world. This mutual respect and support is a crucial piece for this partnership. Time together and time spent alone are equally important. Making decisions together must not be done with expectations and bullying; don't expect your partner to go along with every idea that you present. Instead, be curious and interested in how he or she is thinking and what his or her ideas are. This relationship invites you to be open, with a capital "O," because within the Six of Spades is a strong need to be in control. This inability to yield comes from fear. The opportunity in this relationship is to let go to the unknown and trust the love that your partner really does have for you. Simply put, allow yourself be loved.

If you are in this relationship and finding it challenging, look within yourself to see how those challenges might be manifesting in your relationship with yourself. Then make whatever adjustments are necessary to attain clarity. Usually, the main adjustment required is to give yourself permission to explore the feeling that it's safe to be loved. Once you've done that, you will have greater insight into what your relationship means to you and how much you are willing to stretch yourself for love. Fantasy, as noted earlier, runs quite strongly in the veins of this connection, so be sure that your logic is following your heart rather than your fears. You don't want your logic to override your heart; however, you do want it to be equally represented in the equation. Giving must be a key part of your behavior if you are to reap the greatest rewards of this relationship.

If you are considering getting into this relationship, be sure that you are seeing clearly. Don't make excuses for things you see that you know aren't right or won't work for you. With clarity and the right attitude, you could successfully pick up from wherever you left off the last time you were together.

The Keys to the Kingdom of the Six of Spades

Extend Yourself

Go beyond your attitudes. Explore and discover ways to be more giving, loving, and forthcoming with your partner. This card can have a bit of a self-absorbed streak at times. To avoid having that energy contaminate your connection, make the decision to give more and want less.

Acceptance and Support

Each of you will need to have the freedom to express yourselves as individuals. The Six of Spades has a need to be in control, and that energy will wind through this relationship. So make an effort to be accepting and supportive of your partner as an individual outside the relationship, and let go of any need to be in control.

Sensibility

Remember that this can be a fantasy-driven connection. Make an effort to be practical, pragmatic, and levelheaded. Dreaming is good, and from dreaming comes inspiration; however, you must balance your dreams with what is practical.

Receptivity

Be open and honest, and remember—openness with a capital "O." Receive your partner's ideas and inspirations with curiosity and enthusiasm, rather than the need to be right or in the lead. Let go of your ego if it tries to get in the way—that need for the ego to be in charge is fear based. These types of behaviors will spoil the beauty and sensitivity of your relationship, so don't go there. Remain Open.

46

Seven of Spades

Commitment to Spirit

The Seven of Spades is the mystic, and this is an extremely spiritual influence. Living an unconventional life will be the best way to align with and make the optimal use of this unusual relationship connection. In fact, it was most likely an unexpected or unique situation that brought the two of you together. It's also quite possible that sparks were flying. This is a very electric, magnetic connection. The unique individuality present within this connection definitely warrants recognition. How that distinctive quality will be shared is the question that deserves to be explored.

The Seven of Spades is one of the most spiritual cards in the deck. Reaching for higher values will be a fundamental key to making things work in this relationship. Sevens demand refinement, and if you don't initiate effort in that direction—whether it be mental, physical, or spiritual refinement—you'll create obstacles in your life and in your relationship.

Masterful communication will be needed to navigate the unusual and unexpected realms of this relationship's universe. You will be asked to dive deep within yourself and then deeper into this connection. Nothing less will suffice, and you will learn in unconventional directions as you do so. Judgments and criticism are unacceptable and will create major rifts in the heart of your connection. You will be asked to deal with the phantoms of your past, and you must always expect the unexpected. Get comfortable with the unknown, and learn to let go and relax, because this will be an unusual and extraordinary experience.

If you are now in this relationship, know that it's one that is different from the norm and needs special attention to keep things alive and harmonious. That special attention must come in the form of deep, sometimes serious communication. You must cultivate an ease of being with what is unknown and unseen. Last but not least, you'll have to abandon all tendencies toward judgment and criticism. This connection can be a magical ride on an eclectic wave if you're willing to be guided solely by your inner direction. Use the wisdom of this card to make this experience a valuable one for yourself and your partner. Great emotional maturity can be gained.

If you are considering this relationship as something to step into, read carefully and know that it's not for someone who wants everything to be a certain way and then remain the same. Stability and continuity will not happen here. On the high side, this can be a very powerful spiritual relationship, one in which your past is transformed into your future. There is room for and support of material success with this connection as well, as long as higher values are realized.

The Keys to the Kingdom of the Seven of Spades

Self-Realization

Commitment to a path of self-realization will bring forth the most powerful blessings this card has to offer. Greater self-awareness will be gained from serious introspection and discipline. Excellent mental and spiritual strength will be gained through such choices.

Cultivate Understanding

Understanding is a key element to be fostered in this relationship. Each of you will have enhanced mental creativity by being together, and along with this creativity comes a need for independent expression of self. Honor this need and give way to the higher aspects of the mind in yourself and your partner. At the foundation of your support will be a deep understanding of the importance of having the freedom to fully express one's spirit.

Refinement

Allow yourself to be led by your spirit and your inspiration. Yield the need to be in control, and give way to innocence with your partner. To do this, trust will be necessary. Sevens teach us to be more refined. This one in particular is very demanding in regard to spirituality and the higher realms of thinking. It's a serious card, and it will call forth such energies from within you. If you do not heed the call of the Seven of Spades to go more deeply into your spirit, it will create external obstacles that push you in that direction. It is best to be proactive in your choices.

Relinquish the Past

Liberation from the past, acceptance of the unknown, and openness to the future could be the greatest gifts of this connection. Dwelling on old issues will only create major obstacles. If you are not conscious in this relationship, it will manifest things to wake you up. Let go and embrace that which you have only dreamed of.

47

Eight *of* Spades

The Path of Endurance

T he hand of destiny was at work when this meeting occurred, and the timing probably couldn't have been better. The Eight of Spades is a powerful card of determination and longevity that stands on a foundation of commitment, and this commitment is the very substance that will keep this relationship intact. When things are kept positive, this can be a very empowering connection. And when the two of you move forward with intention, you can accomplish anything you set out to do. As a relationship card, this composite has what it takes to be long lived and successful; you simply have to be clear about the value of the relationship itself and honor that. Both of you have to be certain that this partnership is serving your highest good. Then you must stay focused with that understanding and use your intention to boost each other forward as individuals. It's all about supporting your partner in being all he or she can be, and embracing your personal power to manifest your desired reality.

The Eight of Spades connection usually creates a very stable life, and family is a strong part of that foundation. There will always be new beginnings of some sort manifesting to bring fresh energy and new perspectives into the relationship, so be open and receptive to change, new ideas, and the sometimes-unexpected situations that arise. You will find yourselves reevaluating the connection you have with each other, as well as the value of your being together. In fact, this reevaluation is a necessary part of this relationship, because it keeps you focused on where you are going as individuals and as partners.

Individuality is of utmost importance in this relationship and must be seen as such. When you are on target with yourself and each other and clear about your direction, success will be guaranteed. If you find yourselves stuck or uninspired, innovative thought and the experiences they prompt will move you forward; good fortune will come you way, as well, when you step out into the unknown. The Eight of Spades is a virtuoso at readjusting, evolving, and transforming things when they no longer work. This card is determined to succeed, and it will shape-shift when necessary to do so. It's brilliant. Because of this characteristic, the Eight of Spades energy will make known to you any bad habits or ways to approaching life that do not further your experience in positive ways, so that you can change. *Discipline* is a key word for this card, and being in this relationship might inspire you to be more disciplined. This is a highly intelligent card that knows how to thrive in life.

If you are presently in this relationship, understand that this card demands that you reevaluate and renew your values, your intentions, and your direction on a fairly consistent basis. Joint goals that inspire and motivate are key. You must be open to learning new ways of approaching change and the unexpected, as these things will come about often. Making efforts to bring fresh energy into the relationship will feed your connection and give it new life. Be innovative with your thinking. Your relationship requires fresh energy on a consistent basis, and it's imperative that you make this a priority. When you do, all will be well. When you don't, questions and discontentment arise, as the result of energy stemming from an underlying restlessness that wants to move things forward. If you entertain doubt in this relationship, it will deteriorate the very structure of your connection.

If you're considering this relationship as a possibility for yourself, think carefully about what is being said and understand that this is a very determined type of energy, one that takes work to keep it on track. It's a destined connection, so it's quite possible that you are being given the opportunity to bring more discipline and excellence into your life. By destined, I don't mean that you are without choice about whether or not you choose to be in this relationship. I do mean that it's likely you have a strong connection with one another, and it's most important that you make a conscious choice of how you want to be together now, as there is a reason for your meeting.

The Keys to the Kingdom of the Eight of Spades

Intention

Intention is the key to moving this relationship in the direction that you want it to go. The Eight of Spades is a card of success and endurance. You choose how to manifest this energy. This is not a decision that you make only once. It's a decision that you make every day as you choose to be present in this relationship. This energy demands that you stay alert and present, so that you don't become complacent and miss the opportunities that come with this card. Aligning your intentions about co-creation with the opportunities that present themselves is the key to every kind of success with this relationship.

Adaptability

Open your mind to change, and be flexible with your responses. It's possible there will be events, situations, and opportunities that show up out of the blue. Be prepared by being adaptable and receptive, as these happenings will feed fresh energy into your relationship, like a spring into a river.

Self-Discipline

Individuality is required for you to thrive in this relationship. Your individuality will be cultivated through self-discipline. You'll have plenty of opportunities to practice emotional and mental mastery and self-control—all of which will take you to the higher path of this connection. This card represents successful manifestation as a result of disciplined behavior. That discipline will translate into how you express your personal excellence and will fine-tune your expression, again and again.

Surveyors of Life

Together you will explore and discover the world around you and beyond. Adventures will provide the infusion of energy that keeps this relationship light. Travel is favored, and new experiences will generate great inspiration to nourish your connection and support its growth. Travel and adventure must be on the calendar as often as possible.

48
Nine of Spades
Re-creation and Reinvention

This is a unique and unusual relationship, to say the least. The Nine of Spades represents blessed endings and new beginnings. With this card ruling a relationship, that's exactly what you will get on an ongoing basis. This card influence will demand that you deal with past emotional issues and unpleasant matters of the heart so that you can release them. The new learning gained from understanding the old issues will establish fresh perspectives in your relating and your comfort with true intimacy.

Emotions can be turbulent and drama can be high with this connection. Beginnings, endings, and redefining experiences, similar to miniature deaths and rebirths, will recur. These transformational experiences will repeatedly cause you to re-create yourselves and reinvent your lives. This is likely to continue throughout the span of your time together. Not always, but often, Nine of Spades relationships break up and get back together more than once. This can be a highly emotional connection, and in order to maintain balance you must have clear intentions and exercise your communication with skill and sensitivity. Being conscious and skillful with how you communicate will enable you to harness and manage the emotions that arise between the two of you.

The fiery passion inherent within this connection could very well have been the magnetism that drew the two of you together initially. However, the foundation of this partnership must be built on friendship rather than passion, or it will not succeed or survive. It's possible that your way of living will change significantly when you are in this relationship. The Nine of Spades, being symbolic of loss and letting go, can be a challenging composite unless you willingly ride the ups and downs of this card's temperament and become comfortable with surrendering your ego and willfulness when that is the request that life is making. This influence is highly demanding and most powerful for self-development.

This relationship is not always meant to be long lasting, although it can be. Often your being together is providing time for a completion of some kind between the two of you. It will be in your best interest to be sensitive and consciously aware every step of the way. Consult your inner wisdom via your intuitive intelligence, so that you can be clear about the difference between a learning opportunity and the end of the relationship, if you are in that situation. This can be a challenging connection, so pay attention. It can also be a very beautiful, spiritually enlightening experience, one where you and your partner are extremely expressive with your love and your creativity. However, even in its best form, the Nine of Spades relationship will offer endings as the doorways into new life.

This partnership can bring good financial gain when your individual intentions are aligned with one another and you support each other toward the accomplishment of your chosen goals. You may have to guard against power struggles and battles of the will. Be vigilant, because these struggles—such as hidden agendas—can be very subtle. Rather than being subjective, maintain objectivity, which will give you perspective.

If you are presently in this relationship and experiencing the up-and-down, on-and-off frustrations caused by things not going as you expect them to, you might want to step back and let go of your expectations. Engage in meditation or another form of mental discipline to let go of your old ways of thinking, being, and believing if they are getting in the way. You have to be a good spiritual surfer to ride the waves of this relationship with grace. When you take a path of self-discipline, it will empower you. To reach the highest attributes of this card you must be a student of life itself, breath by breath. Be your partner's best friend, and then his or her lover. The key to self-mastery in this relationship lies in learning to take things impersonally. Tall order? You bet!

If you are thinking about being in this relationship, be aware of what is being said. This connection has the potential to be one of the most difficult connections in the deck, unless you are able to truly be yourself. However, if you are comfortable in your skin and feel happy and free, then step in deeper and see what happens. It's a great connection if you are both dedicated to a spiritual path. Remember that communication and friendship are the keys to experiencing happiness in this relationship.

The Keys to the Kingdom of the Nine of Spades

Friendship

First and foremost, friendship must be at the foundation of this relationship. This will create the stable base of trust necessary for your connection to ride its course. Embrace the gift of having your partner in your life by honoring him or her as your dear friend. The genuineness initiated by this embrace of friendship will permeate your entire relationship.

Self-Discipline

Cultivate self-discipline and practice mastery with your mind and emotions. Commitment is the key to achieving self-mastery. You will notice distinct differences between the times when you are making effort toward self-discipline and the times when you're not. This difference of perception will be most noticeable in your mental-emotional states of mind. This cultivation of self will promote clarity in your communication with your partner.

Surrender

Surrender your ego and let go of the past. Embrace each moment as it arrives. This card represents death and rebirth, endings and new beginnings, and these experiences lead to the re-creation of yourselves and the reinvention of your lives. These transformational cycles will be a constant in this relationship.

Receptivity

Choose to be receptive to and supportive of your partner's personal power. Be attentive and aware of how his confidence is actually a reflection of your own, or how her inhibitions are a calling from within you. This mirroring works both ways between you. And this card asks us to become bigger in our lives and greater with who we are. We accomplish this by letting go of and going beyond the fear-based boundaries we've established for ourselves. The Nine of Spades requests the death of the ego so that we can be reborn into innocence; it asks us to let go of fear and trust life. When we abide by the rules of this card, we will experience the gifts it has to give. Being in this relationship is a spiritual initiation.

49

Ten of Spades

The Path of Achievement

The Ten of Spades symbolizes the power of accomplishment—accomplishment that comes from hard work and a lot of it. There will be obstacles to overcome with this relationship life path, and there will be much to achieve. Often with this influence, one's personal life can be sacrificed for the sake of accomplishment in career. The need to balance career or work with home life might show up as a challenge. Harmony will be found by making your personal lives and your careers equal priorities. If these needs don't show up in the practical sense, they will show up in the communication between the two of you. The Ten of Spades is a somewhat self-focused character, and you're likely to find yourself dealing with issues regarding selfish behaviors. These conflicts can be advantageous if you're on a path of personal transformation and self-development. However, if you are looking for a relationship that is easygoing and relaxed, that's not what you will find here.

This card symbolizes material and spiritual attainment. If these things represent the goals you have for yourself in life, this relationship will offer you tremendous support by providing opportunities that further your attainment. If necessary, the energy of this card will force you to let go of any ways in which you are holding back from life. In order for this relationship to thrive, you will have to let go of old disappointments and fears regarding love, because they will clutter your mind and get in the way of the progressive movement that is the natural energy of the Ten of Spades.

You must take care to avoid overcommitting your time to work, other people, or things that don't directly nurture you. Full throttle ahead and commitment to whatever the focus may be in the moment can be a theme with this card at the helm. The relationship has great potential for the two of you working together in business. Balance will be required for this relationship to have peace and harmony at its core, and travel and leisure time will create that balance. A loving connection that is fully expressed is a must. In order for you to access deep levels of intimacy in this relationship, you have to spend quality, quiet time together sharing your dreams and ambitions. Plan little getaways to stimulate your minds and your passion.

Whatever your ambitions may be for yourselves and your partnership, realize that this relationship will take diligent work and serious commitment for it to be a healthy, happy, and rewarding one.

If you're already in this relationship, hopefully this information will help you better understand it. Know that the dynamics outlined here will always be present with this connection. How you choose to use the innate characteristics of this card will determine the success of your connection. You may have to let go of how you think things should be. If you rise to meet the challenges gracefully, you'll experience the good fortune this relationship has to offer. If you're resistant to the changes that come your way, you will experience disappointment time and time again. This relationship is designed to encourage a commitment to personal growth. There's not room for victims in this relationship. You are being asked to participate 100 percent. Give it your all, and it will give back to you tenfold.

If you're thinking about stepping into this relationship, be sure that you're up for the challenge; it's not an easy connection. But if the two of you are working together for a specific goal or purpose, it can be ideal. The Ten of Spades will ask you to rise to a more mature expression of your emotional intelligence, and in this partnership you'll become stronger emotionally and clearer about how you want to express yourself in a relationship.

The Keys to the Kingdom of the Ten of Spades

Shared Goals

Working together will fuel the flames of passion that reside deep within the belly of this connection. Whether this work be for the good of others, a personal goal, or in business, you will multiply your odds for success tenfold by doing things as a team. Teamwork applies to supporting one another with personal goals as well.

Emotional Maturity

Clean up old emotional patterns and be more consciously aware in your relating. This relationship will support you in becoming more mature in your emotional expression. The Ten of Spades does not tolerate drama. Call on your wisdom when issues arise, and transform whatever is going on by taking time to understand the source of the problem. Don't let old patterns contaminate the relationship. This card influence is more than capable of encouraging and supporting you to grow emotionally.

Self-Awareness

It's through the cultivation of your self-awareness that you will experience the greatest gifts this card has to offer in a relationship. Engage in a variety of activities outside your mundane responsibilities. Doing so will enhance your self-expression as individuals. Self-awareness and continued growth toward personal enlightenment are sure ways of keeping this connection fresh and alive. Complacency will not do with this connection.

Expressions of Affection

Be generous with your expressions of love and affection whether they be small gestures of appreciation or grand displays of adoration. You must let your partner know on a daily basis, one way or another, how much you love him or her. You are both going to want to feel the gloriousness of your love—you will crave this. Take the time to bask in your love.

50

Jack *of* Spades

Spiritual Initiation

If you're looking for tradition, you won't find it here. However, if you like drama and constant change, you've come to the right place at the right time. Truth be known, this meeting could not have been prevented without a major catastrophe or something of equal persuasion getting in the way. It was destined to take place. The question is, are you up for the ride?

The Jack of Spades is the card of the actor or the thief. The highest expression of this card is that of the spiritual initiate. He's a brilliant master of disguise. The ways in which his cleverness manifests in your relationship will depend on the road the two of you choose to travel, and you may have a recurring opportunity to make this choice. You're bound to wear a variety of hats and many different costumes in this jack's kingdom, so if you're looking for consistency, look again.

This relationship is powered by pure will. The willful nature of this card can manifest as stubbornness and fixed attitudes that will show up in both your verbal and nonverbal communication. Harboring ill feelings or withholding your love will conjure the deceptive nature of this card. These types of behaviors must be kept in check, and how you do that is through open, honest sharing with one another. There's no room for hidden agendas in this partnership; they are like land mines for the environment of your love.

The way to establish and maintain the most pristine expressions of this brilliant card is through your shared creative ventures.

Whether you're supporting one another in your individual efforts or creating things together, the two of you working side-by-side as partners will lift the heavy seriousness that may show its face at times in this relationship. Work connected with health, healing, medicine, or spirituality can be very rewarding; however, anything that you choose to do can be utterly successful when you align with the brilliance of this jack. If you do work together, it will stabilize the unpredictable characteristics of this influence, so it might be wise to find something, even if it's on the sidelines, to spend time doing as a team. It's possible to make a lot of money with this card ruling the kingdom; it just takes determination, hard work, and a united effort of support.

You must let go of old stories from the past regarding relationships. Old patterns and ideas will get in the way and cause unrealistic scenarios time and time again—this is where the drama comes in. This connection will offer you great opportunities to embark upon a totally new way of being in a partnership. To take advantage of these transformative experiences you must be open like a small child, moment-by-moment, and willing to wear the many different hats and costumes that will be presenting themselves for you to try on. This could actually be fun as long as you let go of any need to be in control, which would come from fear.

No one survives a power struggle in this kingdom. The law of this land states that you take responsibility for your actions by employing the highest integrity with yourself and others. If you choose otherwise, negative energies will come onto the stage of this production and act out their villainous characteristics right before your eyes.

Play is the key. Play is the secret. Play is important for this to be a happy experience, because getting stuck in ruts and being too serious about things will deteriorate this relationship at light speed.

Applied intelligence and an inner conviction that knowledge is power are the underlying factors for success. Rising to the higher aspects of this card can bring great good fortune in personal endeavors and in business ventures. Education is key, and any new learning, especially together, will bring the greatest rewards.

If you're in this relationship, take to heart the knowledge that you are riding on a very high wave of extremely acute mental perception that holds within it an innate wisdom about dancing with life in the moment. Living in this relationship without that awareness will create frustration and disappointment. You have most likely called this experience to yourself for a higher initiation into your intelligence and raw spirituality. To reap the greatest benefits of this connection, commit to that initiation and let go of your past self.

You may have to beware of deception with this card; if any question of deception comes up, it's likely that you're onto something, so pay attention and be honest with yourself. However, this card's strong element of drama can make something out of nothing, so clarity and good discernment are key elements for assessment. This is a very demanding relationship. The demand is to become more conscious. If you are already self-aware, you can become more self-aware. You can also take your personal creativity to an exalted realm of expression.

If you are considering embarking upon or exploring this connection as a possible relationship, search within yourself for the part of you that seeks to leave your unwanted past and move into a new way of being—mentally, emotionally, and spiritually. Know that this jack will bring forth your willfulness and any stubborn behaviors that you normally can keep at bay, and that you will have to deal with these things in a more confrontational way. All relationships are mirrors that allow us to see ourselves more clearly. This one can be exciting, and if you like drama, it can be great. Be sure that you are seeing this relationship clearly for what it is, as this card's deceptiveness can cause us to ignore things that we would otherwise pay close attention to. Ultimately, the Jack of Spades is a highly creative energy that moves quickly and changes form. If that sounds exciting to you, let your adventurous spirit take you for a ride on the magic carpet of the Jack of Spades.

The Keys to the Kingdom of the Ten of Spades

Adaptability

You must be willing to be flexible and changeable in this relationship. Allow yourself to explore new aspects of yourself that have not been expressed before. Chances are you will have many opportunities to go beyond your comfort zones, stepping into new territories of self-expression and relationship. Take advantage of these opportunities by letting go of old self-concepts.

Knowledge Is Power

Assume the power embodied in this connection and ride the high road to acquire its greatest gifts. You have everything to gain when you access the creative power that is locked within this card. Apply your greatest intelligence, your most cultivated wisdom, and your deepest desire to love in all new ways. Your intention will be everything. And with this jack in charge, your intentions will manifest at light speed, as long as they are in alignment with right timing. Be. Do. Enjoy.

Create What You Want

Together you can create anything imaginable, and your imaginations will most likely be working overtime. So enjoy the inspiration and take action with your ideas. Those ideas could easily find their way to fruition and lead to good fortune. Mutual support of self-expression is number one, and being lovers and friends comes second. This jack is an individual, and the individual must be supported first in this relationship. Outward expressions of support go a long way in this relationship, so remember to take time and make an effort to find new ways to express your love and appreciation. Working together on projects can be very profound and extremely rewarding.

Be Open and Let Go

Due to the strong dramatic characteristics within this relationship, emotional issues are very likely to come up, and you have to deal with them for what they are—usually fear stemming from past experiences. If you don't consciously work at letting go of the past, the relationship will be contaminated by things that have nothing to do with it. This is the card of spiritual initiation, so you must consciously and continuously initiate yourself into a higher level of awareness. Take that responsibility seriously, and you will experience tremendous self-growth. Ignore it, and you will be unhappy. The key to letting go of the past is to bravely be open to the present moment, with the totality of your being.

51
Queen of Spades
The Path of Self-Mastery

The Queen of Spades is one of the highest royal cards in the deck. In fact, she is second in command only to the all-powerful King of Spades. Unfortunately, the power of this card is not often realized and is thus wasted in menial tasks and subservient ways, which aren't really suitable for the queen. This card has the power to manifest whatever it chooses, as long as there is an awareness of what is possible and a mental intention toward what is desired. This power must be used with intelligence and integrity for outcomes to be positive.

This queen is destined to serve humanity in the highest spiritual ways. However, hard labor is more often the resulting experience and may be something you will want to avoid in your relationship. If you don't assume the power of this queen to be the master of her destiny, the relationship will be a constant processing of issues, emotional upheavals, and misunderstandings that emerge from a lack of clear personal intention for what is truly desired. On the high side of things, if you take a more global and consciously aware approach, this could be a very powerful experience for both of you. This is a challenging relationship connection unless you are very dedicated to becoming more self-aware, or unless the two of you are committed to some greater global cause through religion, spirituality, medicine, humanitarian efforts, or things similar. The bottom line for this connection is that you have to share strong spiritual values.

This is a unique and unusual relationship composite, and it will be imperative that you draw on your intelligence to deal with your emotions; otherwise, things will become totally insane and very difficult.

Most likely, there was a feeling of immediate knowing when you first met, or maybe the circumstances that you met under were unusual in some way. Whatever the case may be, it's certain that you've known one another before, in another lifetime perhaps, and you're picking up where you left off last time you were together. But that was then, and this is now. The question is, where are you now, and what are your choices related to being together?

It's important to understand that both of you at times will likely be a bit willful and possibly stubborn in your interactions with one another. Unless you turn this powerful energy toward a common goal, and become more open and receptive rather than wanting to always be in command, you will create misery and hard work for yourself, your partner, and your relationship.

Speaking of hard work, there will be no end to that. This card represents labor. Whether you are living the royal side of the card or not, you will be working hard, and you will benefit from any effort you make, whether it be spiritual or material. This queen embodies a strong material desire, so there may be a need to balance extravagance with practical thinking when it comes to money and spending. Finances can be a real issue if you don't stay on top of your priorities. Meditation or some other practice of self-discipline will help to keep your priorities in perspective.

If you are presently in this relationship, schedule time together for enjoyable activities. Be open and receptive in your communication, and draw on your intelligence and logic rather than your emotions when facing problems that arise. The communication in this relationship can reach cosmic realms as long as you have shared values and joint goals for your life together.

If this is a relationship you are interested in, think clearly and use sound logic as you get to know each other. It's not the person that might be a challenge; it's the connection and energetic composition that's created when the two of you come together. This relationship can take tremendous effort for some, and it's not the best path for a relationship unless the two of you are like-minded and work together for a common goal; when this is true, however, you will be blessed beyond belief.

If you are presently in this relationship and any of these challenges are showing up, use the advice given here, apply the Keys to the Kingdom for this card, and see what happens. This is not a doomed relationship by any means. And depending on your personal cards and how they relate in your life paths, it's possible that they can offset this queen's energy and make the relationship easier.

The Keys to the Kingdom of the Queen of Spades

United Efforts

Common goals and joint efforts will actually strengthen your bond of love. This queen is known as the mother of humanity, and when she is engaged in joint efforts, she shines brightly. Find a cause and support it together, or work as a team in a business. Whatever your personal goals may be, and however you choose to work in the world, at the very foundation of your relationship there must be mutual support and loving respect.

Realistic Goals

Strive for the highest and best for yourself and others, personally and professionally. Set priorities to live by, spiritually and materially. However, don't make things burdensome. Spades are about building foundations. Through self-discipline and hard work, you can build foundations that are strong and sturdy, and you want to remain realistic with what you can actually do. The Queen of Spades can have a tendency to want to save the world. Best not to go there with your relationship. Maintain a balance in your perspectives that supports the priorities that you've chosen for yourselves.

Self-Discipline

Use a practice of self-discipline, such as meditation, to keep your mind and emotions, as well as the day-to-day tasks of life, in check. Spades symbolize self-discipline, and when we are engaged in spade relationships, discipline becomes the magic that keeps life running smoothly and opens the doors of opportunity.

Lightness of Heart

Stay light and be playful together to keep things uplifted and open between you. Exploration and shared adventures of the mind are important for this queen. Create a warm, nurturing living environment to support the innate sensitivity of this queen's energy and her preference for beauty. Home will be your sanctuary, the place where the rest of life comes into perspective.

52

King of Spades

The Power of Mastery

Seen as the most powerful card in the deck, the King of Spades is the ruler of the entire kingdom. This king possesses pure, unadulterated power. If you have already entered into this relationship, you are in the process of being initiated into a higher realm of your own conscious awareness, whether you know it or not. If you're not aware of this, you might want to take a look in that direction, because this card says that it's time to upgrade your perspective and adopt a greater way of viewing who you are and what you're aware of relative to life itself.

If you are thinking about entering this relationship, know that you will be made aware of any limiting personal beliefs, outdated ways of thinking, and unconscious behaviors that you have. Resisting this awareness will cause you misery. This is no lightweight connection. It's a powerful ride in the royal kingdom of the cards. Spades represent spirituality and wisdom; on the higher or more aware side of things, they can open you up to new perceptions and align you with the deeper parts of your being. On the negative or unconscious side of things, the spade suit will create obstacles and difficulties for you to surmount until you catch on. You determine your outcomes by how you choose to respond and by the actions you decide to take. This king rules the spade suit, and he plays a very strong game of "Who wants to become enlightened?"

Your most valuable tools for being in a relationship will be your self-awareness and self-discipline. Discipline combined with discernment will bring out the greatest qualities of this card.

Learn how to make the best choices for empowering yourself and your partner, and the floodgates of blessings will open and give way to a new relationship with life for both of you. The possibilities for change and new beginnings are abundant in this king's domain. Ambition will evoke strength, and actions and intentions will lead to excellence. The King of Spades will naturally upgrade your intentions.

On the lighter side of things, there is an element of this relationship composite that is playful, fun loving, and curious about life. Expressions of love and playful affection are most vital for the playful side of this card; the desire for these elements will be strong and must be well fed. Traveling together, outdoor activities, and eclectic adventures should be high on the priority list. Time spent together in these ways will balance the restless energy inherent in this king. Conventional ways of relationship will not work here, so if you're looking for tradition, you might want to look elsewhere. This connection is eclectic, unusual, and extremely powerful for the individual. Embrace the opportunities that it offers rather than trying to manipulate them.

Stimulating conversation, new learning, exploration, and the exchange of new ideas are keys for keeping your connection alive and healthy. Feelings of uncertainty or confusion can arise with this connection; when these feelings occur, they are signs that letting go and greater communication and understanding are needed to move forward. You have to move beyond your old emotional patterns, fears, and insecurities to be wholly in this relationship, and you can bet that those old issues will come up while this king is sitting on the throne.

A challenge that can present itself is one of power struggles or ego battles. This king wants things his way, and that willfulness will be brought forth in each of you. To transform this energy, you must actively and intentionally empower one another's individuality. Remember, this is not a traditional type of relationship; independence is the key to each of you being happy and to your relationship having longevity. When you feel resistance, when you have the urge to overpower or control, or when you choose to shut down emotionally, realize in that moment that you're making the lesser choice for yourself and the relationship. Step back and ask yourself how you can empower your partner by supporting him or her to be a greater individual; supporting your partner toward his or her personal signature of self-expression is a must.

If you are presently in or drawn to this King of Spades relationship, know that, deep down inside, you are longing to free yourself from old behavioral patterns and beliefs that no longer serve you. Some part of you is asking to be liberated and taken into a greater awareness of self and being, as well as a greater expression of who you are. This is not the easiest relationship to be in; however, it can be one of the most rewarding for attaining spiritual and material accomplishment and a new lease on life.

The Keys to the Kingdom of the King of Spades

Self-Awareness

Self-awareness must be your first priority. You must do your best to be present in each moment, as fully as possible, as this will reveal new insights into yourself and life. This is a powerful connection for a relationship. The dynamics that occur must be observed with conscious awareness and taken seriously; otherwise, challenges can seem insurmountable. It's not only a love relationship—it's a spiritual initiation as well. If you don't value this aspect of your connection together, old fears and ghosts from the past are likely to torment you.

Spiritual and Material Accomplishment

Spiritual and material accomplishments are at the top of the list of priorities for this king and are available for you to manifest as realities. Efforts made in these directions can bring great satisfaction and unlimited abundance. Ambition is very important to this king, so you have his blessings to make things happen. All effort will be handsomely rewarded.

Adventures in Creation

Adventure has got to be a priority, and by adventure I mean exploring new forms of self-expression as individuals and as a couple. New locations, new ideas, new people, and new ways of doing things will stimulate the curiosity and creativity of this card. Within this king lives an insatiable desire for life that must be fulfilled with variety and spice. These new explorations will inspire and delight you, and take your relationship with one another to new heights of awareness and pleasure.

Connect Your Thoughts

The independent nature of this king can lead to isolated moments of self-reflection and, oftentimes, a simple desire to be alone. Support these times, and then resume with the communication and conversations that are the lifeblood of this connection. Old ways of communicating, or communicating from unconscious places that are nested in the past, will not fly in this relationship. Here you are asked to become more authentic, communicative, and interesting, and in doing so you will survive the scrutiny of this king's power. Be creative!

53

The Joker

The Unknown Journey

When the sum of your personal cards combined equals 53, the Joker governs your relationship. The Joker symbolizes alpha and omega. He stands at both the beginning and end of time, and he is the bridge between the past and the future. This card influence is eclectic, filled with creative genius, and can be very unpredictable. All of these characteristics will be present in your relationship.

The unknown and the unpredictable will be strong elements that can manifest in your communication with one another, so take care that you are actually saying what you intend to communicate, hearing what the other is actually saying, and saying what you actually mean. Each of you will be inspired to reach beyond any limitations you have set for yourself. Anything can and most likely will be created and attained, and your goals should be easy to accomplish with this card ruling the kingdom of your relationship. This is very fast-moving, eclectic energy that can make a relationship feel a bit like a whirlwind at times.

Because the Joker symbolizes the beginning and the end, it acts as a bridge between the first and the last cards in the deck, the Ace of Hearts and King of Spades. Therefore, these two cards are strong influences in the Joker relationship. To understand the full spectrum of their influence, please read the information for the Ace of Hearts and the King of Spades, and apply the Keys to the Kingdom from each of those composite cards to your Joker relationship.

Reference Charts

What's Your Card?

DAY	JAN	FEB	MAR	APR	MAY	JUN	JUL	AUG	SEP	OCT	NOV	DEC
1	K♠	J♠	9♠	7♠	5♠	3♠	A♠	Q♦	10♦	8♦	6♦	4♦
2	Q♠	10♠	8♠	6♠	4♠	2♠	K♦	J♦	9♦	7♦	5♦	3♦
3	J♠	9♠	7♠	5♠	3♠	A♠	Q♦	10♦	8♦	6♦	4♦	2♦
4	10♠	8♠	6♠	4♠	2♠	K♦	J♦	9♦	7♦	5♦	3♦	A♦
5	9♠	7♠	5♠	3♠	A♠	Q♦	10♦	8♦	6♦	4♦	2♦	K♣
6	8♠	6♠	4♠	2♠	K♦	J♦	9♦	7♦	5♦	3♦	A♦	Q♣
7	7♠	5♠	3♠	A♠	Q♦	10♦	8♦	6♦	4♦	2♦	K♣	J♣
8	6♠	4♠	2♠	K♦	J♦	9♦	7♦	5♦	3♦	A♦	Q♣	10♣
9	5♠	3♠	A♠	Q♦	10♦	8♦	6♦	4♦	2♦	K♣	J♣	9♣
10	4♠	2♠	K♦	J♦	9♦	7♦	5♦	3♦	A♦	Q♣	10♣	8♣
11	3♠	A♠	Q♦	10♦	8♦	6♦	4♦	2♦	K♣	J♣	9♣	7♣
12	2♠	K♦	J♦	9♦	7♦	5♦	3♦	A♦	Q♣	10♣	8♣	6♣
13	A♠	Q♦	10♦	8♦	6♦	4♦	2♦	K♣	J♣	9♣	7♣	5♣
14	K♦	J♦	9♦	7♦	5♦	3♦	A♦	Q♣	10♣	8♣	6♣	4♣
15	Q♦	10♦	8♦	6♦	4♦	2♦	K♣	J♣	9♣	7♣	5♣	3♣
16	J♦	9♦	7♦	5♦	3♦	A♦	Q♣	10♣	8♣	6♣	4♣	2♣
17	10♦	8♦	6♦	4♦	2♦	K♣	J♣	9♣	7♣	5♣	3♣	A♣
18	9♦	7♦	5♦	3♦	A♦	Q♣	10♣	8♣	6♣	4♣	2♣	K♥
19	8♦	6♦	4♦	2♦	K♣	J♣	9♣	7♣	5♣	3♣	A♣	Q♥
20	7♦	5♦	3♦	A♦	Q♣	10♣	8♣	6♣	4♣	2♣	K♥	J♥
21	6♦	4♦	2♦	K♣	J♣	9♣	7♣	5♣	3♣	A♣	Q♥	10♥
22	5♦	3♦	A♦	Q♣	10♣	8♣	6♣	4♣	2♣	K♥	J♥	9♥
23	4♦	2♦	K♣	J♣	9♣	7♣	5♣	3♣	A♣	Q♥	10♥	8♥
24	3♦	A♦	Q♣	10♣	8♣	6♣	4♣	2♣	K♥	J♥	9♥	7♥
25	2♦	K♣	J♣	9♣	7♣	5♣	3♣	A♣	Q♥	10♥	8♥	6♥
26	A♦	Q♣	10♣	8♣	6♣	4♣	2♣	K♥	J♥	9♥	7♥	5♥
27	K♣	J♣	9♣	7♣	5♣	3♣	A♣	Q♥	10♥	8♥	6♥	4♥
28	Q♣	10♣	8♣	6♣	4♣	2♣	K♥	J♥	9♥	7♥	5♥	3♥
29	J♣	9♣	7♣	5♣	3♣	A♣	Q♥	10♥	8♥	6♥	4♥	2♥
30	10♣		6♣	4♣	2♣	K♥	J♥	9♥	7♥	5♥	3♥	A♥
31	9♣		5♣		A♣		10♥	8♥		4♥		JOKER

Solar Values of the Cards

A	♥	1	A	♦	27
2	♥	2	2	♦	28
3	♥	3	3	♦	29
4	♥	4	4	♦	30
5	♥	5	5	♦	31
6	♥	6	6	♦	32
7	♥	7	7	♦	33
8	♥	8	8	♦	34
9	♥	9	9	♦	35
10	♥	10	10	♦	36
J	♥	11	J	♦	37
Q	♥	12	Q	♦	38
K	♥	13	K	♦	39
A	♣	14	A	♠	40
2	♣	15	2	♠	41
3	♣	16	3	♠	42
4	♣	17	4	♠	43
5	♣	18	5	♠	44
6	♣	19	6	♠	45
7	♣	20	7	♠	46
8	♣	21	8	♠	47
9	♣	22	9	♠	48
10	♣	23	10	♠	49
J	♣	24	J	♠	50
Q	♣	25	Q	♠	51
K	♣	26	K	♠	52

Spirit and Soul Card Chart

BIRTH	SPIRIT	SOUL	BIRTH	SPIRIT	SOUL
A♥	A♦	3♥	A♦	2♦	A♥
2♥	A♣	A♣	2♦	6♣	A♦
3♥	A♥	Q♣	3♦	6♥	Q♦
4♥	4♠	10♠	4♦	5♠	5♥
5♥	4♦	5♣	5♦	9♦	3♣
6♥	4♣	3♦	6♦	9♣	3♠
7♥	8♥	3♥	7♦	9♥	9♥
8♥	7♠	7♥	8♦	Q♠	7♣
9♥	7♦	7♦	9♦	Q♦	5♦
10♥	J♣	5♠	10♦	Q♣	Q♠
J♥	J♥	J♥	J♦	3♠	J♣
Q♥	10♠	9♣	Q♦	3♦	9♦
K♥	2♣	9♠	K♦	3♣	7♠
A♣	2♥	2♥	A♠	7♥	2♣
2♣	A♠	K♥	2♠	6♠	K♣
3♣	5♦	K♦	3♠	6♦	J♦
4♣	5♣	6♥	4♠	10♣	4♥
5♣	5♥	4♣	5♠	10♥	4♦
6♣	8♠	2♦	6♠	9♠	2♠
7♣	8♦	J♠	7♠	K♦	8♥
8♣	8♣	8♣	8♠	K♣	6♣
9♣	Q♥	6♦	9♠	K♥	6♠
10♣	J♠	4♠	10♠	4♥	Q♥
J♣	J♦	10♥	J♠	7♣	10♣
Q♣	3♥	10♦	Q♠	10♦	8♦
K♣	2♠	8♠	K♠	K♠	K♠

♥ Planetary Ruling Cards

A♥
12/30 - 3♠

2♥
12/29 - 2♦

3♥
11/30 - 5♣   12/28 - 3♦

4♥
10/31 - 8♦   11/29 - 6♣   12/27 - 6♠

5♥
10/30 - 9♦   11/28 - 7♣   12/26 - 5♦

6♥
10/29 - 10♦   11/27 - 8♣   12/25 - 6♦

7♥
9/30 - 5♠   10/28 - K♦   11/26 - 9♣   12/24 - 9♠

8♥
8/31 - 6♣   9/29 - 6♠   10/27 - A♣   11/25 - 10♣   12/23 - 8♦

9♥
8/30 - 7♣   9/28 - 5♦   10/26 - K♣   11/24 - J♣   12/22 - 9♦

10♥
7/31 - 5♥   8/29 - 10♦   9/27 - 8♠   10/25 - 3♠   11/23 - A♦   12/21 - A♦

J♥
7/30 - 6♥   8/28 - 9♣   9/26 - 9♠   10/24 - 2♦   11/22 - K♥   12/20 - K♥

Q♥
7/29 - Q♣   8/27 - 10♣   9/25 - 8♦   10/23 - 5♣   11/21 - 5♣   12/19 - 3♥

K♥
6/30 - 6♦   7/28 - 8♣   8/26 - K♦   9/24 - 6♥   10/22 - 6♥   11/20 - 4♠
12/18 - 2♦

♣ Planetary Ruling Cards

A♣
5/31 - Q♣ 6/29 - 7♦ 7/27 - 7♥ 8/25 - Q♣ 9/23 - 10♠ 10/21 - Q♣
11/19 - J♥ 12/17 - 3♦

2♣
5/30 - K♣ 6/28 - 6♣ 7/26 - 8♥ 8/24 - K♣ 9/22 - K♣ 10/20 - J♦
11/18 - 6♠ 12/16 - 4♦

3♣
5/29 - 3♠ 6/27 - 9♦ 7/25 - J♣ 8/23 - 3♠ 9/21 - 3♠ 10/19 - 9♥
11/17 - 7♠ 12/15 - 5♦

4♣
4/30 - J♠ 5/28 - 2♦ 6/26 - 10♦ 7/24 - 10♥ 8/22 - 10♥ 9/20 - 2♦
10/18 - J♠ 11/16 - 8♠ 12/14 - 6♦

5♣
3/31 - 7♥ 4/29 - A♠ 5/27 - 3♦ 6/25 - 9♣ 7/23 - J♥ 8/21 - J♥
9/19 - 3♦ 10/17 - A♠ 11/15 - 9♠ 12/13 - 7♦

6♣
3/30 - 10♣ 4/28 - Q♥ 5/26 - 6♠ 6/24 - A♣ 7/22 - A♣ 8/20 - 3♥
9/18 - 6♠ 10/16 - Q♥ 11/14 - Q♣ 12/12 - 8♦

7♣
3/29 - J♣ 4/27 - Q♠ 5/25 - 5♦ 6/23 - K♣ 7/21 - K♣ 8/19 - 2♣
9/17 - 5♦ 10/15 - Q♠ 11/13 - J♦ 12/11 - 9♦

8♣
3/28 - 10♥ 4/26 - 4♠ 5/24 - 6♦ 6/22 - A♦ 7/20 - A♦ 8/18 - A♥
9/16 - 6♦ 10/14 - 4♠ 11/12 - Q♦ 12/10 - 10♦

9♣
1/31 - 4♣ 2/29 - 2♦ 3/27 - 2♦ 4/25 - K♥ 5/23 - 9♠ 6/21 - 2♦
7/19 - 2♦ 8/17 - 4♣ 9/15 - 9♠ 10/13 - 2♥ 11/11 - J♠ 12/9 - K♦

10♣
1/30 - 10♠ 2/28 - 5♠ 3/26 - 3♥ 4/24 - K♠ 5/22 - 8♦ 6/20 - 8♦
7/18 - 5♦ 8/16 - 10♠ 9/14 - 8♦ 10/12 - K♠ 11/10 - 3♦ 12/8 - A♣

J♣
1/29 - 4♥ 2/27 - 4♦ 3/25 - 2♣ 4/23 - 7♠ 5/21 - 9♦ 6/19 - 9♦
7/17 - 4♦ 8/15 - 4♥ 9/13 - 9♦ 10/11 - 7♠ 11/9 - 2♠ 12/7 - K♣

Q♣
1/28 - 7♦ 2/26 - 5♠ 3/24 - 3♦ 4/22 - 5♣ 5/20 - 5♣ 6/18 - 10♠
7/16 - 5♠ 8/14 - 7♦ 9/12 - 10♠ 10/10 - 5♣ 11/8 - J♥ 12/6 - A♠

K♣
1/27 - 6♣ 2/25 - 6♠ 3/23 - 4♦ 4/21 - 4♥ 5/19 - 4♥ 6/17 - J♦
7/15 - 6♣ 8/13 - 6♠ 9/11 - J♦ 10/9 - 4♥ 11/7 - Q♥ 12/5 - 2♣

♦ Planetary Ruling Cards

A♦

1/26 - 7♣	2/24 - 5♦	3/22 - 3♣	4/20 - 3♣	5/18 - 5♥	6/16 - Q♦
7/14 - 5♦	8/12 - 7♣	9/10 - Q♦	10/8 - 5♥	11/6 - Q♠	12/4 - 3♠

2♦

1/25 - 10♦	2/23 - 8♠	3/21 - 6♦	4/19 - 6♦	5/17 - 8♣	6/15 - J♠
7/13 - 8♠	8/11 - 10♦	9/9 - J♠	10/7 - 8♣	11/5 - A♥	12/3 - 4♠

3♦

1/24 - 9♣	2/22 - 9♦	3/20 - 9♠	4/18 - 7♦	5/16 - 7♥	6/14 - A♠
7/12 - 9♠	8/10 - 9♣	9/8 - A♠	10/6 - 7♥	11/4 - 2♥	12/2 - 5♠

4♦

1/23 - 10♣	2/21 - 8♦	3/19 - 8♦	4/17 - 6♣	5/15 - 8♥	6/13 - 2♦
7/11 - 8♦	8/9 - 10♣	9/7 - 2♠	10/5 - 8♥	11/3 - K♠	12/1 - 6♠

5♦

1/22 - K♣	2/20 - J♦	3/18 - J♦	4/16 - 9♦	5/14 - J♣	6/12 - Q♠
7/10 - J♦	8/8 - K♣	9/6 - Q♠	10/4 - J♣	11/2 - 4♥	

6♦

1/21 - A♦	2/19 - Q♦	3/17 - Q♦	4/15 - 10♦	5/13 - 10♥	6/11 - 4♠
7/9 - Q♦	8/7 - A♦	9/5 - 4♠	10/3 - 10♥	11/1 - 5♥	

7♦

1/20 - K♥	2/18 - K♥	3/16 - K♦	4/14 - 9♣	5/12 - J♥	6/10 - 5♠
7/8 - K♦	8/6 - K♥	9/4 - 5♠	10/2 - J♥		

8♦

1/19 - 10♠	2/17 - 5♣	3/15 - 3♦	4/13 - A♣	5/11 - 3♥	6/9 - K♠
7/7 - 3♦	8/5 - 5♣	9/3 - K♠	10/1 - 3♥		

9♦

1/18 - 4♥	2/16 - 4♦	3/14 - 2♠	4/12 - K♣	5/10 - 2♣	6/8 - 7♠
7/6 - 2♠	8/4 - 4♦	9/2 - 7♠			

10♦

1/17 - 5♥	2/15 - 3♣	3/13 - 3♠	4/11 - A♦	5/9 - A♥	6/7 - 8♠
7/5 - 3♠	8/3 - 3♣	9/1 - 8♠			

J♦

1/16 - 6♣	2/14 - 6♠	3/12 - Q♥	4/10 - 2♠	5/8 - 4♦	6/6 - 4♥
7/4 - Q♥	8/2 - 6♠				

Q♦

1/15 - 7♣	2/13 - 5♦	3/11 - Q♠	4/9 - 3♠	5/7 - 3♣	6/5 - 5♥
7/3 - Q♠	8/1 - 5♦				

K♦

1/14 - 8♣	2/12 - 6♦	3/10 - 4♠	4/8 - 2♦ -	5/6 - 4♣	6/4 - 6♥
7/2 - 4♠					

♠ Planetary Ruling Cards

A♠

1/13 - 9♣	2/11 - 9♠	3/9 - 2♥	4/7 - 5♠	5/5 - 7♦	6/3 - 7♥
7/1 - 2♥					

2♠

| 1/12 - 10♣ | 2/10 - 8♦ | 3/8 - K♠ | 4/6 - 6♠ | 5/4 - 6♣ | 6/2 - 8♥ |

3♠

| 1/11 - J♣ | 2/9 - 9♦ | 3/7 - 7♠ | 4/5 - 5♦ | 5/3 - 7♣ | 6/2 - 9♥ |

4♠

1/10 - A♦	2/8 - Q♦	3/6 - 5♥	4/4 - 8♠	5/2 - 10♦

5♠

| 1/9 - K♥ | 2/7 - K♦ | 3/5 - 6♥ | 4/3 - 9♠ | 5/1 - 9♣ |

6♠

1/8 - 3♥	2/6 - A♣	3/4 - Q♣	4/2 - 8♦

7♠

| 1/7 - 4♦ | 2/5 - 2♠ | 3/3 - 8♥ | 4/1 - J♦ |

8♠

1/6 - 3♣	2/4 - 3♠	3/2 - 9♥

9♠

| 1/5 - 4♣ | 2/3 - 2♦ | 3/1 - J♠ |

10♠

1/4 - 7♦	2/2 - 5♠

J♠

| 1/3 - 10♦ | 2/1 - 8♠ |

Q♠

1/2 - K♣

K♠

| 1/1 |

About the Author

Sharon is known for her amazing accuracy with this system of timekeeping, and for her clear delineations of birthdays as associated with the playing deck. As an internationally known life consultant, award-winning author, and third-generation clairvoyant, Sharon has worked with thousands of people from around the world and from all walks of life.

A natural-born mystic, Sharon Jeffers has since childhood seen the future, heard the thoughts of others, and perceived things that others cannot. She began her studies in numerology and astrology at age thirteen and began doing readings spontaneously with the regular deck of playing cards at age twenty-one. She has been a student of this Mystic Science of the Cards since 1990.

Sharon has more than twenty-five years of experience in transformational healing work, applied kinesiology, and Black Hat Feng Shui. She has created and facilitated training methods for both enhanced performance and behavioral modification for police, prison inmates, at-risk and special-needs kids, educators, parents, athletes, health professionals, and corporate management teams. She founded the Center for Integrated Learning and Excelerated Learning Strategies.

As the author of several books, including this latest work, she is frequently heard on radio stations nationwide. Her client list includes police departments, educational institutions, people from around the world, and celebrities. She lives in Los Angeles and does much of her consulting over the phone. Please see her website at www.starofthemagi.com.

Hampton Roads Publishing Company

. . . for the evolving human spirit

HAMPTON ROADS PUBLISHING COMPANY publishes
books on a variety of subjects, including
spirituality, health, and other related topics.

For a copy of our latest trade catalog,
call toll-free, 800-766-8009, or send your name and address to:

HAMPTON ROADS PUBLISHING COMPANY, INC.
1125 STONEY RIDGE ROAD · CHARLOTTESVILLE, VA 22902
e-mail: hrpc@hrpub.com · www.hrpub.com